The Lead Machine

The Small Business Guide to Digital Marketing

Rich Brooks

Dedication

I happily dedicate this book to my two daughters, Maya and Sophie, who never would have spoken to me again if I didn't dedicate this book to them.

(Now girls, will you please tell me where the remote is?)

More Praise for The Lead Machine

Rich Brooks gets it. Sure, lots of people write books about marketing. But few people are actually grinding it out everyday with real businesses creating real results. That's what impresses me about Rich. He's not just a "sayer." He's a "doer." And if your small business follows the principle taught herein, I know it's going to lead to some exceptional results in an age where many are being left behind.

Marcus Sheridan
Author of They Ask You Answer: A Revolutionary Content Marketing Strategy

* * *

While there are plenty of digital marketing books out there, few put together all the pieces to help entrepreneurs build a platform, attract and audience, generate leads, and measure everything effectively. The Lead Machine is that book. If you want to build your business online, you're already holding the guide you'll need.

Amy Porterfield
Social Media Strategist and Author of Facebook Marketing All-In-One for Dummies and

***

Rich Brooks is a small business owner and understands the pulse of digital marketing. He put together 20 years of experience into a simple-to-follow guide makes it a must-read for all entrepreneurs and marketers who need to understand that lead generation is the life blood for all companies.

Sue B. Zimmerman
Instagram Marketing Expert

***

For busy small business owners and entrepreneurs, getting consistent results with your online marketing can be such a challenge in today's fast-moving digital world. Look no further than The Lead Machine as your fabulous new guide. Rich Brooks walks you through a proven step-by-step process that is easy to follow and will generate measurable results, including how to increase your search engine ranking, how to engage your audience on social media, and most importantly, how to generate more leads and sales online. With 20 years of experience working with small businesses, Rich has the first-hand experience of what works online, and he's documented it all here in a comprehensive and practical manner.

Mari Smith,
Premier Facebook Marketing Expert
Author The New Relationship Marketing, and coauthor
Facebook Marketing: An Hour A Day

***

This is THE new handbook for entrepreneurs looking to get found via search engines, drive qualified traffic to their site, and generate more business online. If you've been struggling to grow your online business, The Lead Machine is something you need to deep-dive into - it'll help. Plain and simple!

Chris Ducker
Author of Virtual Freedom

***

You can try a lot of things and see what works, or you can take the advice of Rich Brooks. I'd bet on this guy any day of the week.

Chris Brogan
Author of The Freaks Shall Inherit the Earth:
Entrepreneurship for Weirdos, Misfits, and World Dominators
and Co-Author of Trust Agents: Using the Web to Build
Influence, Improve Reputation, and Earn Trust

***

Too many small business owners know the internet is critical to their growth and success, but they have no plan and just end up throwing spaghetti at the wall to see what sticks. In The Lead Machine, Rich Brooks lays out a process that anyone can follow to build their business and become successful.

Jaime Masters
Author of The Eventual Millionaire: How Anyone Can Be an
Entrepreneur and Successfully Grow Their Startup

***

Small businesses need to know how to generate more leads online to compete against bigger and more well-funded competitors out there. In The Lead Machine, Rich Brooks breaks down exactly how business owners, entrepreneurs, and marketers can reach and engage their customers online. This is a must-read for any small business owner looking for a game plan to stand out and to drive leads.

Shama Hyder
Author of The Zen of Social Media
Marketing and Momentum

***

If you want an easy-to-understand guide to generating more attention and leads online, that will help your business grow over time...this book is for you. Just good, simple advice for business owners that want more revenue. If that's you, buy it, read it, do it.

Joe Pulizzi
Author of Content Inc: How Entrepreneurs Use Content to Build Massive Audiences and Create Radically Successful Businesses and Epic Content Marketing

***

Most companies are on the web. No big deal, but Rich Brooks, in his easy to follow guide, helps turn your website into a cash machine and that's a Big Deal!

Norm Brodsky
Co-Author of The Knack: How Street-Smart Entrepreneurs Learn to Handle Whatever Comes Up and Street Smarts: An All-Purpose Tool Kit for Entrepreneurs

***

Praise from Clients and Associates...

Rich Brooks has just published "The Lead Machine: The Small Business Guide to Digital Marketing", a reflection on 20 years of providing digital marketing projects to small businesses. This book is truly worth reading. Rich has been in the trenches of digital marketing; he 's got real depth of knowledge. I've attended many of Rich's numerous presentations at Agents of Change and others in recent years and I can say that he really knows how to explain vital, current issues in the fast changing digital marketing field. He's got a sense of humor that is refreshing and it serves to make his presentations fun, but also to drive home digital marketing points. He's been a guest speaker in a class of mine at the University of New England and the students have enthusiastically commented how much they valued his visit. This book won't let you down.

Tom Leach
Certified Business Advisor
Maine Small Business Development Center
Professor of Marketing
University of New England
Biddeford and Portland, Maine

***

So many small businesses see the promise of the internet and digital marketing, but don't know how to harness the power of these tools. Enter Rich Brooks and The Lead Machine, the x The Lead Machine

perfect guide for entrepreneurs who are looking to generate more leads and business from the web.

Mark Delisle
State Director at Maine Small
Business Development Centers

***

Rich is "Mr. 1's and 0's" in the Portland market. Years ago when I built my first web site with Flyte I recognized a company built with talented individuals who would stay on top of technologies as they evolve and Rich's group has done just that. Fun, interesting and always looking out the front windshield.

Bentley Collins
Marketing Director, Sabre Yachts

***

After working with Rich Brooks and his team at flyte, I know that this is more than just talk. Rich understands how business grow and generate business from the web and he distills it all into this book. If you're looking for a guide to help you navigate these waters, look no further than The Lead Machine.

Jim Shiminski
Principal at DAC Sales

***

I've had the pleasure of working with Rich Brooks and flyte new media over the years at a number of different companies. He has an uncanny ability to take a problem and provide a solution that innovative and more simple to implement. Over the years, Rich has not only been a valuable business partner, he has been a digital media mentor. He understands where small businesses are coming from, what their goals are, and how to help them accomplish those goals. His 20 years of experience are on display in The Lead Machine, and any small business can benefit from picking up this book and putting his advice to work.

Jason Schlosser
General Manager at Turnkey Vacation Rentals

***

In today's world, yesterday's marketing just does not work. Rich Brooks and the flyte team brought innovative digital marketing strategies to my business, increasing website traffic, conversions, and bookings. Rich is ingenious, and his thought-provoking, fun and stimulating personality is what brings his work — and this book — to life! Sure to help you and your business thrive, Today's Digital Marketing is a must read for today's small business owners!"

Judy Moore
President, Canine Behavior Counseling, LLC

Table of Contents

Introduction

Years ago, I was at my favorite lunch spot, Market Street Eats in Portland, Maine. I was waiting for my wrap and chatting with the owner, Colin, when a woman walked in. You could sense that this was her first time there, and being somewhere between lunch and dinner, it was pretty quiet. In other words, there was no line or other indication of how the ordering process might work.

She walked up to the counter and one of the new wait staff greeted her warmly and asked if she wanted to see a menu. Colin seemed unimpressed. I wondered why—after all, it was a friendly greeting.

He explained, "I told those guys to go around the counter, show a new customer the big sandwich board, make some recommendations, hand her a take-out menu, and ask questions. But they think it's crazy to spend that much time for a $7 wrap."

"Ah," I replied, "but it's not a $7 wrap. It's $7, once a week, 52 times a year for 10 years. Plus, she might tell her friends, too."

"Agreed. We look at it that way because we own our own businesses," Colin replied.

Colin went on to tell me about one of his first jobs, selling men's suits. "'**Never let the customer get ahead of you in a sale**,' my boss would tell me. 'The customer doesn't know as much as you do. He doesn't work here. Once he gets ahead of you in the sales process everything falls apart.'"

******

Years later, Colin's brother Kyle directed a romantic comedy with zombies—a RomComZom, if you will—that I got a bit part in as a "featured zombie."

It has nothing to do with this book, but I thought it was an interesting aside.

******

This is a book about generating quality leads online. So you may wonder why I started with a story about selling $7 wraps.

The point is that digital marketing is less about digital and more about people. It's about providing guidance throughout the process. Whether you're engaging with someone on social media, writing a helpful blog post, showing how to accomplish something on YouTube, or directing them to the resources they need on your site, your job is to guide them.

By offering help and assistance throughout the process, you'll win more fans, generate more leads, and ultimately make more sales.

This Book

It seems like every business book I've read over the past couple of years has an opening chapter that sets out to explain why this book is important. Why this topic is important. Perhaps, even, why this author is important.

If you're running your own business, or if you're in charge of marketing for a business, then this book is valuable, if not necessarily "important." *Moby Dick* was important. *War and Peace* was important. *50 Shades of Grey* was drivel. This book, if you put it into action, will prove valuable.

The topic is important. Businesses need leads like fish need water. And smaller fish to eat. And these days, most people do their research online. At the end of 2014, *Adweek* reported that 81% of shoppers do research online before buying a product. In 2015, Mintel reported that 72% of opinion-seekers age 25-34 look to social media contacts for recommendations when purchasing goods and services.

If you don't have a strong digital presence, if you're not present where your audience "hangs out" online, then your competition is going to take that business from you.

As far as the author's importance...well, he's important to his two kids. And their cat.

Shifting to first person, I've been doing this digital marketing thing since 1997. I've worked with hundreds of companies and non-profits to get their websites up and running, and drive traffic with SEO (Search Engine Optimization) and social media. I've presented to thousands of people over the years, and even run my own conferences all about search, social, and mobile marketing.

Important? Your call. Experienced? Definitely. Invested in helping you succeed? Absolutely.

The typical introduction then goes on to talk about who this book is for. It's usually a very narrow group, like "Everyone who has a job, is looking for a job, or whose name is Job." Or, "Men between the ages of 18 - 79 and the women who love them."

Then they talk about who the book is *not* for. It's usually not for people looking for a get-rich-quick solution. It's not for people who talk loudly during movies. It's not for people serving time in a federal penitentiary. Or the women (and men) who love them.

Who This Book is For

This book, *The Lead Machine*, is for people who run their own small to medium-sized business (SMB), or have a marketing role in the business. It's for social media managers, directors of business development, and digital marketers.

It's written for people who run "real" businesses. What I mean by that is that in my twenty years of running a digital marketing agency, we've worked with bed & breakfasts. Furniture makers. Yacht builders. Business consultants. Medical practices. Dog trainers. College entrance consultants. Natural food stores. Marinas. Software creators. And local banks and credit unions.

Although most of the examples and language are about SMBs, they also apply to non-profits, as long as they have an entrepreneurial mindset. "Clients" could be stakeholders, volunteers, members, or donors. Or even legislators.

Who is this book not for?

It's not for get-rich-quick-on-the-Internet people. Most of the tactics and strategies in this book take time to fully develop.

While you may see some results quickly, it will take an invest-ment in time and energy to really be successful.

It's not for people who think Internet marketing is a magic bul-let, or a "set it and forget it" solution. Digital marketing is too crowded and too competitive for that to work any longer, if it ever did.

Why I wrote this book

In the end, I wanted to write the book that I wish I had when I was first starting out. Something that gave me a framework. Something that broke down a lot of moving parts into pieces that I could understand and put into action.

I wanted to write a book that showed people the necessary steps to start generating high-quality leads that would help grow their business.

I also wanted to encapsulate what I have learned from twenty years of building websites, optimizing them for search engines, engaging in social media, blogging, podcasting, creating videos for YouTube, running webinars, and email marketing.

I hope you find it valuable on your journey to running a more successful business.

Extras

Any book on digital marketing runs the risk of being out of date by the time it gets printed. To avoid that, I'm focusing on more evergreen strategies and tactics in this book, rather than tricks that will expire quickly. I've also included some links to online resources that will be updated as necessary.

Some of these links go directly to the source, others require that you sign up at the site to download some additional resources that will make your life easier and your workload lighter.

This, of course, is called a "lead magnet" and it's a great way for businesses to build their email list.

And that, dear Reader, is lesson #1.

The BARE Essentials of Digital Marketing

In the nearly 20 years I've been doing this, working with hundreds of entrepreneurs, small businesses, and non-profits, I've realized that no matter how unique your business or offerings are, there are certain things that are true for almost every business that wants to succeed online.

You need a website.

You need to drive the right people to that website.

You need some of those people to contact or buy from you.

You need to measure your results.

It really is as simple as that. And as complicated as that, too, because of what it takes to make those simple rules work for you and your business.

These facts have evolved into a framework that I use when working with businesses called **The BARE Essentials of Digital Marketing**. Here's the breakdown:

Build: It starts with a mobile-friendly website designed for results. Designed to get visitors to fill out your contact form, pick up the phone, or click on a "buy now" button.

Attract: You'll need to drive qualified traffic to your site using search engine optimization, social media, and digital advertising.

Retain: To stay in communication with your customer after they leave your site, you'll need to get them to opt into your email newsletter, engage with them on social networks, or follow them around the web with retargeting.

Evaluate: By reviewing your website analytics, email reports, and social media metrics, you can see what's working and what's not, giving you the opportunity to continually improve your results.

In the following sections of this book, I'll be going into detail about each of these elements, and how you can use them to build your business online.

Build

Build a better mousetrap and the world will beat a path to your door.

— *Ralph Waldo Emerson*

The first part of the BARE Essentials is Build, where we talk about how to build a website that builds your business.

But this section is not for designers looking for bleeding edge design ideas and whether to use Parallax design (Don't.). Nor is it for developers looking to improve their coding ability or to learn the newest language or platform.

This section is for you: the small business owner or the marketer responsible for attracting your ideal customer, for generating leads, and closing sales. Although a mousetrap may have negative connotations (especially if you're a mouse), the idea of attracting and converting your customers is what this section is all about.

We're going to determine who you can help and how you can help them. You're going to build a platform where they can get answers to their questions and solutions to their problems. You're going to make the site so easy to use it's frictionless.

Your site is going to speak to the concerns of your site visitor. It's going to establish trust. It's going to guide your visitor to success. Now, let's get started.

Getting Started

Do I really need a website?

Over the years, I've heard people say that you don't need a website. That all you need is a blog, or a Facebook business page, or a LinkedIn profile, or a single page on a vendor's site.

I have no idea where those people are now.

While I can't predict the future (the first time I saw email I thought it was the stupidest thing I had ever encountered and stated out loud that no one would use it), in today's business environment, ***you need a website.***

Your website is your home on the web. It's where business happens. It shows you're credible and believable. After all, you wouldn't expect to do business with someone out of the back of a truck, right?

Unless they were selling ice cream. Or tacos. Or Korean BBQ. And even then, it's really the side of a truck.

Your website is where you *warm* leads. Where you can leverage things like social proof, authority, and expertise. Where you can build your list, generate leads, and sell stuff.

No matter how big and powerful a platform like Facebook gets, it's not the place to build your business. It's not "your" property. You're building on someone else's land. At any time, that landlord can change the rules. Take away your voice. Make you pay to reach your community. Kick you out.

And there's nothing you can do about it.

Not that you shouldn't be using social platforms. Just like networking events in real life, or IRL as the kids say, they are an important space to grow your audience and make connections.

But, would you walk around a networking event, greeting people with an unsigned contract asking them to do business with you? Probably not. You'd spend your time getting to know people, getting to know their business and their problems, and then seeing if you're a good fit.

If they needed help, and you were in a position to help them, then you might invite them back to your office to talk business.

In this scenario, Facebook or Twitter is the networking event, and your website is your office. That's where you hold court and have home field advantage.

Your digital marketing will fail if you don't have a place to bring people.

Your website serves as a place to drive traffic, entertain, educate, and inform your guests, and move people down your sales funnel.

In this chapter we're going to take a look at what you need to get a professional, effective website up and running.

What do I need to get a website up and running?

Chances are you already have a website, but it you don't, this is what you'll need:

A domain name.

This is how people (and Google) find you on the web. You can find Apple at http://www.apple.com. You can find flyte new media at http://www.takeflyte.com.

You don't want people to have to find you at someplace like mycompany.wix.com or mycompany.wordpress.com. While people (and Google) *can* find you there, you're not building up trust by building on someone else's property. That's because wix.com and wordpress.com are the "root" domains in those examples. You are just a subdomain. No one wants to do business with a subdomain.

If Wix or WordPress (in this example) ever went out of business, you'd disappear. No forwarding address. Nothing.

Similarly, if *you* decide to move, all the trust you built up at that domain—at that location—would stay behind.

To register a domain, you'll want to use a Domain Registry company like GoDaddy (GoDaddy.com) or Network Solutions (NetSol.com).

ProTip: Register your own domain if you can. If you can't, make sure the domain is under your name and control. I've seen some businesses struggle to get their domain name back because an unscrupulous (or perhaps unpaid) web developer registered the domain under their own name and refused to give up control.

A hosting company.

This is the company that makes your website available to your prospects and customers. When someone types in your URL (web address), finds you on Google, or clicks a link to your website, your hosting company provides the appropriate files that make up your website.

Hosting companies charge from nearly nothing to several thousand dollars per month, depending on your needs. Things that can drive up the cost of monthly charges include how many big files you have (audio, video, etc.), how secure your site needs to be, how many other people share the server with you, whether you need special hosting for e-commerce, the level of service, and more.

Many small businesses try and save money by going with a hosting company that charges under $10/month. After twenty years in this business, I strongly recommend *not* going with the cheapest option.

Because when things go wrong—and they always do—cheap hosting companies are impossible to reach. And if you're lucky enough to get some big publicity, like getting on Oprah, they can't handle the inevitable traffic so they'll shut you down to protect themselves and the people who also have space on their server.

For most small businesses, you can go with the hosting recommendation of your web developer. It's likely that they use this host a lot, know where all the important files are stored, and can build out your website more quickly and affordably when they know what to expect.

A digital agency.

You don't actually *need* a digital agency. Just like you don't actually *need* an accountant. Or a car mechanic. Or a heart surgeon.

OK, maybe you need the heart surgeon. You know, in case of emergency.

However, and I'm biased here, working with the right digital agency is a great investment in the success of your digital marketing. And in case you're not familiar with the term "digital agency," it's simply a company that does creative digital work for other businesses, often building websites and handling digital marketing.

Usually it includes a few important people:

- **A web designer.** This is the person who knows how to design beautiful, professional websites. They understand how people are likely to interact with your site, what colors will have specific meaning to your visitors, what photos will engage them, and where to put calls action to increase interactivity. Most importantly, they know not to use Comic Sans.
- **A web developer.** This is the person who builds out the site. They might do it in HTML, or they might use

a Content Management System (CMS) like WordPress or Drupal. They know how to make the slideshow move automatically (or not), set up your gallery, make your online forms deliver leads to your inbox, get your site to load faster, and make it mobile friendly.

- **A programmer.** If there is custom programming required to make sure your website accomplishes your business goals, this is the person who will make it happen. With the web platforms available today, many things that used to require a programmer no longer do. However, if the platform or plugins can't do exactly what you need them to do, a programmer can create something from scratch.

- **A digital marketer.** This person runs keyword analyses to uncover the most important words you should use on your website and where to put them. They find out where your audience hangs out online and builds social media profiles there. They run Adwords campaigns so that when your ideal customer is Googling something, they see your ad first. They run Facebook ads where they narrowly target your perfect customer and create engaging ads that lead those potential customers to your website or opt-in page. They understand whether you need to be blogging, podcasting, creating online video, or hosting webinars. And they help you with all of these things. Depending on the size of the agency, this may be one person or dozens, each with their own specialty.

- **A copywriter.** This person writes all of your copy based on the keyword analysis that the digital marketer did. And they know how to write copy that will rank well and persuade your site visitor to take a desired action on your site.

- **A photographer.** When stock photography isn't right, or isn't enough, this person will take photos that you can use on your website, blog, email newsletter, social media profiles, slide decks, and print material.

- **A videographer.** Whether you're posting videos to YouTube for marketing purposes or creating information products to sell on your site, this is the person who understands lighting, blocking, tackling, editing, and how to make the most of each video.

- **A project manager.** This is the person that puts it all together. Usually he or she is your main point of contact. They shepherd the project through to completion, making sure that things are done on time and on budget, or that if changes to scope, budget, or timeline are necessary, that everything is communicated to all parties.

Now, not all agencies will have someone in all these positions. Many agencies may use contractors to accomplish certain tasks, such as copywriting or photography. Other agencies might have a focus on videography, so they may include an entire team of people that put some small independent filmmakers to shame!

Here's why you may want to hire a digital agency to help you build and market your website:

- **An agency knows how to build a website quickly and efficiently.** They've done it before. By letting them build it out, you don't need to spend your time learning the basics of a specialty they've already mastered. Instead, you can spend that time working on your business.

- **They are a team of experts.** To create the most effective web presence possible, you need to cover a number of areas of expertise. Design, development, programming, SEO, copywriting, social media, and email marketing/list building, just to name a few!

- **It's unlikely that web design and development is part of your company's core competency.** As any successful business person will tell you, focus on what you do best and outsource the rest. Building a website is something you will only need to do every five years or so, and the process will change completely before you need to do it again. So why waste your time learning a skill you'll only need once when you can be using that time to drum up business, serve customers, and send out invoices?!?

And if you have your site built on a CMS (content management system), which we'll discuss shortly, then you'll be able to update and maintain the site easily, even if someone else built it for you.

How do I choose a digital agency?

Start by doing some research. Ask some friends who run businesses or have gone through this process recently. They will probably have some recommendations for you.

You can also ask this question publicly on Facebook, but this does come with some risks. One of your friends may be a web designer and pressure you to use them even if they're not the best fit for your business. Friends and family often make for terrible vendors and customers. There are of course exceptions, but those are...exceptions.

Or worse, they may have a nephew/brother-in-law/babysitter who is building websites and strong arm you into using them! The only thing worse than hiring family is hiring the family of a friend. If you have already hired your best friend's nephew, may your experience be different.

You may also want to Google it. If you want to work with a local company, you could try searching for "Santa Barbara web design" or "Maine WordPress developer" as appropriate.

If you've seen a site that you like, often you can track down the agency behind it. Sometimes they include their name or even a link at the bottom of the page. If not, it's possible the company who owns the site will share that information with you...assuming they're not your direct competition.

As you start to collect names of agencies, be sure to check out their websites. Do you like the look of their site? Do you like the look of their portfolio (the other websites they've designed)?

Do they have a blog, podcast, or some resource area? (As you'll see in later chapters, I'm a huge proponent of developing a content marketing strategy to establish credibility and help make you the obvious choice for your ideal customer. To that end, you should be looking for digital agencies that understand this and practice it as well.)

If you need an agency to help you with writing copy, ask yourself if you like the flow and "voice" of their copy. If you're looking for someone to do your video marketing, do they have high quality videos on their site? If you need someone to help you rank well in the search engines, did they appear on the first page of Google when you searched?

Try and narrow the potential agencies down to three to five by the time you're ready to contact them. You want to be able to compare and contrast, but if you have too many choices, you'll never move forward. If you're meeting with a dozen different agencies, then reviewing and comparing twelve different proposals, you'll be spinning your wheels for months.

Ultimately, getting a website built is not like buying a toaster at Target. It's not a simple exchange of money for product. Instead, it's a relationship that could last several months for a simple website to several years for ongoing marketing and maintenance.

If an agency comes with lots of recommendations but you just don't personally click with them, keep searching. This isn't an arranged marriage and all the Yelp reviews in the world won't make up for a disconnect between you and your web partner.

Why an RFP is bad for your business.

Many companies use RFPs (request for proposals) to gather proposals, get pricing, and compare "apples to apples." In certain industries, especially in government, it may be a required step in the process.

It's been my experience, however, that in web design and digital marketing, they are counter-productive.

First, digital marketing is new enough that it can be difficult, if not impossible, to compare apples to apples. One agency claims they include SEO, the other one doesn't. However, the "included" SEO may just be installing a widget...something the second agency does without claiming it as SEO.

Secondly, many established agencies won't respond to RFPs because they can be easily sent to dozens of firms and posted on the requesting company's site and in public forums. What tends to happen with RFPs is they attract the agencies with the least experience and the most free time.

From the agency's perspective, it feels less like a first date and more like they were just dropped into the Hunger Games!

What questions should I ask a digital agency?

Congrats! At this point you should be down to three to five agencies you think might be a good fit. Reach out to these agencies and schedule a time to meet.

The goal here is to get a sense of:

- Do they have the experience to pull off a successful project?
- Do you click with them and their approach?
- Can you afford them?

Remember that a good agency is also trying to uncover whether you'll be a good fit for them. They may do their best work on lead gen (lead generation) sites or really shine on e-commerce. They may prefer a certain vertical, such as hospitality, or work only with non-profits.

Here are some good questions that I've received over the years (that you can feel free to borrow):

Have you ever worked with a [insert business type or industry vertical] before?

This question gets to the heart of whether the agency has experience in pulling off similar projects in the past. Interestingly, some businesses prefer that an agency has experience in their vertical while others won't do business with an agency that has worked with their competition.

In my experience, as long as the agency keeps you in your own private silo and doesn't share confidential information, it's a positive thing that an agency has experience in your or a similar industry.

What is the process to launching a website?

Every digital agency has their own process for planning, developing, and launching a website. Having them walk you through the process can help you understand how everything will unfold.

What platform do you build on?

Many agencies have one or two platforms they prefer for building websites. It could be an open source solution like WordPress, it could be hosted solution like SquareSpace, it could be a private label platform they built themselves, or it could be just traditional HTML, although that's less and less an option.

The platform matters because some platforms have a monthly service fee that could be anywhere from $20 a month to several thousand, so make sure you understand this. Also, if an agency has built their own platform, you won't be able to leave that agency and take your website with you. If you're on a platform like WordPress or SquareSpace, however, you can always switch to another agency that offers those platforms if you decide your agency isn't a good fit any more.

Are your websites mobile friendly?

This is critical. Every agency should be building mobile-friendly websites. If they don't, thank them for their time, walk out, and cross them off your list. Different agencies may have different approaches to mobile, but the most popular, most forward-thinking process at the time of this writing is something called Responsive Web Design (RWD).

Do you offer SEO?

An important question if you're interested in driving qualified traffic from Google and other search engines. Some agencies don't offer SEO, but they may have a partner that provides these services.

If SEO is critical to your success, dig deeper. Ask about their process, what tools and software they use, and what successes they've had in the past.

Do you offer email marketing?

As you'll see throughout this book, I feel every small business can benefit from a healthy, engaged email list. Do they offer email newsletter design? Which Email Service Providers (ESP) do they work with and recommend? (It's a rare agency that doesn't use a platform like Constant Contact or MailChimp.) Do they have responsive email templates? (Reading email is one of the top activities on a mobile device; if your email isn't mobile friendly, people will just click delete without reading it.)

Do you provide digital advertising services?

As search and social have become more competitive spaces, small businesses need to realize the advantages of targeted digital ads. Some popular platforms currently include Google Adwords and Facebook ads.

Like SEO, this is a service that an agency should either have in house, or have the ability to bring in a partner or contractor to get this work done.

Do you provide social media services?

It's rare that a small business won't be doing some social media marketing to connect with their customers and drive traffic. This is a big part of most small business's online success plans.

Do you design logos?

You may not need logo design, but if you do....

Are we responsible for our own photography?

All sites need good photography. The photos for your site can come from your collection, a photographer you or the agency hires, or stock photography. Buying stock photography or hiring a photographer will usually be an additional cost.

Are we responsible for writing our own copy?

Some agencies will write all your copy for you, especially if they're providing SEO services. Others will just take your copy as is and paste it to the site. Make sure you understand what's included and what costs extra.

Do you offer hosting?

All websites need to be hosted somewhere. Does the agency offer hosting? Do they have a preferred host? What type of access will you have to the hosting company if you're going through the agency? Do they have 24/7 tech support, or do all requests have to go through an agency that may only be open 9-5, Monday through Friday?

Also, what type of backup services are provided?

Will you set up all of our emails?

Especially if you're moving hosts, your emails will need to be reconfigured. Will the agency handle this for you? Will they provide you with the information you need so you can check your email on your smartphone as well as your desktop computer?

What might cause this project to go over in time or budget?

This is a GREAT question! I love it when people ask this of me. It acknowledges that projects can go over, but gets to the heart of how can we prevent this.

Common overages might include client delays, requests for additional rounds of design, or changes in scope.

How many websites have you built?

Again, this goes to experience. Now, *someone* has to be an agency's first customer, but are you willing to be that guinea pig? An agency with dozens or hundreds of projects under its belt shows that it has the systems in place to complete the project, but that experience may come at a higher cost to you.

What are your strengths as an agency?

Each agency has their own perceived strengths: design, marketing, video, cost/value, and so on. Do their strengths match up with your needs?

What are your weaknesses?

Nobody wants to admit their weaknesses, but no agency can be everything to everyone.

Are all the people who work on the project employees or do you work with contractors?

Does this matter to you? Do you want to know that all the people who work on your project will sit in the office? Or that they all work in state, or in your home country? Or does it just matter that the agency is ultimately responsible for all their work?

Who will be my main point of contact?

Regardless of the size of the agency, you should have ONE point of contact you can count on during the process. You may have meetings with the designer, developer, and marketing team, but this person—often called the Project Manager—will be the person responsible for communication and keeping the project on time and on budget.

How long will the whole process take?

Web design projects can take from a few weeks (unlikely) to several months. Add in things like SEO and other digital marketing plans and that timeline can quickly expand.

What type of ongoing support do you offer?

You want to work with an agency that's looking for a long-term relationship, which means servicing your account. Will they make updates to your website? Will they upgrade you to the latest version of the software? Will they run scans to make sure no one has hacked your website? Will they provide regular feedback and suggestions on new marketing ideas that could help grow your business?

How will we keep the website up to date?

You *really* want to have your website built on a Content Management System (CMS). That way you can handle most updates yourself. For example, with WordPress you can add, edit, or delete pages. Upload photos. Embed a video. Change the navigation. Blog. Add new features such as a calendar or a photo gallery without understanding any code.

Most small businesses should be able to handle all their own updates if they choose.

Will we get trained in how to make our own updates?

While most CMS platforms are easy to use, any new software can feel intimidating, especially if you see yourself as technically challenged. The agency should be able to provide training for you.

Will we own the website once it's completed?

Some agencies put you on a platform where you don't really own the website. You may own the copy (words) and pictures, but you can't pick it up and take it with you. If this is important, make sure you ask this question.

Can you provide some references for me to speak to?

Most agencies will be able to provide references. And undoubtedly they'll all sing the agency's praises. Find a few companies in the agency's portfolio that they DIDN'T give you as references if you want to dig a little deeper.

How will we communicate during the project?

Will you get weekly emails? Phone calls? Skypes? Do they use Slack (a popular communication software as of this writing)? Is there a project management software the agency uses?

Do you need in-person meetings? Some agencies are more comfortable with virtual meetings, or want to host any meetings to keep costs down.

How much will this all cost?

The agency will probably need to understand exactly what you need before they can provide a quote, and they may need to do some discovery to get you an accurate price. Sometimes that will take a few minutes, and for more complex projects it could take days, or even weeks.

What are your payment terms?

Each agency has their own payment terms. Often you can negotiate if you don't want to pay a big lump sum. Since the project may take 3-6 months, maybe suggest a monthly payment plan.

What questions should I be asking you that I haven't?

I love this question! (I ask it of almost every company that comes in my doors looking for a website or some digital marketing help.)

Can't I do this myself?

If despite all I've said, you still want to build your own website, then have at it! :) There are plenty of platforms, books, tutorials, and how-to videos on YouTube. This isn't rocket surgery: plenty of people have learned how to build their own websites.

The only remaining question for you is: Is this the best use of your time?

If I might make some recommendations on what to keep in mind:

Build it on a CMS. Chances are you'll want to easily update the website yourself, and have your employees be able to update it as well. My personal recommendation is WordPress.

WordPress is the world's most popular platform for building websites because of its ease of use and scalability (ability to grow with your business.) Plus, there are thousands of plugins—little programs that enhance the functionality of WordPress that are available for free or for a reasonable fee.

Choose a template (or theme) that is mobile-friendly. Most new WordPress themes are "responsive," meaning that they optimize themselves for whatever screen size your visitor comes to your site with. Currently, RWD is my recommendation for building mobile-friendly sites. Most up-to-date CMSs have responsive templates, or themes, as they're called on WordPress.

Don't scrimp on hosting. People often like to save on hosting. *Why should I pay $20-$50 or more for hosting each month when I can get it for $5?* If these hosting packages, and the companies behind them, were the same, they would be right. However, the differences can't always be seen until things go wrong.

And as I mentioned before, they always go wrong.

What to do next

Whether you decide to "roll your own" or hire a professional or agency to get your website built, the next section will help you build out the most successful website possible. Remember: if you are hiring an agency, this is a relationship. This is also *your* business. You should come to the party as prepared as possible.

Planning for Success

You don't start a journey without knowing where you're going. Well, unless it's one of those walkabouts or other personal enlightenment journeys, but this is your business we're talking about, so it's time to get focused.

There are several aspects to the "pre-game" of building a successful site:

- Understanding who the website is for
- Understanding their problems
- Understanding how you can help them
- Understanding what you should measure

If you haven't yet, please download the Lead Machine companion workbook at theleadmachinebook.com/workbook. If you go to the Planning for Success section, you'll be able to work on your own successful website.

The questions and statements that follow will help you develop a strategy for success. I've broken them into categories focused on your company, your design, and your marketing. These are based on the client intake sheet that we have developed for our own projects.

Your Business

What is the primary function of your business?

Pretty straightforward: what do you bring to the market place? Do you provide pizza, travel, or bookkeeping services? Another way to think about it: what would someone Google to find your business if they didn't know your company name? I.e., "Boston flatbread delivery," "guided bicycle tours," or "small business bookkeeping company."

What are your top three business goals?

You may have more or less, but more than three and they start to get diluted. "To make more money," is too vague. Try using SMART goals:

- Strategic
- Measurable
- Attainable
- Relevant
- Time-Bound

"To generate five hundred qualified home buyers through our website within six months of launch" would be a much more effective goal.

Who is your target audience?

This is a place where too many businesses fail. I've been told, "employers, employees, and people looking for a job." So, um, basically everyone who's not retired? "Oh, them too."

Or the guy who ran a restaurant and said, "Everyone who needs to eat to survive."

Funny? Possibly. But for a single Tex-Mex restaurant in South Portland, Maine, that doesn't serve breakfast or booze, I think you could have narrowed it down just a wee bit, no?

See how narrow you can make this target audience, even if you feel you may be excluding some of your potential clients or customers.

That restaurant may have been better served by targeting middle-income families within five miles of South Portland who like Tex-Mex food and often go to the mall or the movies on the weekend.

John Lee Dumas, the Entrepreneur on Fire, taught me about developing a business avatar. This is the embodiment of who your ideal customer is. You can give him or her a name, a job, an address, a favorite hockey team, the way she likes to pass her Saturdays or how many hours a day he spends playing Call of Duty.

Marketing to this avatar helps you focus your message, and it will still attract people who don't match up with this avatar.

If you're interested in learning more, listen to my interview with John on *How to Unleash Your Business Avatar* at theleadmachinebook.com/avatar

What are your site visitor's goals when they come to the website?

Where most people fail on this question is that they mistake it for what THEY want out of their audience, not the other way around.

- They want to learn more about my products and services.
- They want to meet my staff.
- They want to buy from me.

While some of these may be true, it might not be the first thing that your customer is thinking when they come to your site.

If they've got grubs destroying their lawn, their goal is to get rid of the grubs and get back their healthy lawn. Whether you or the next company has the right solution, they really don't care.

Now, if you've got an organic solution and your competition doesn't, then you might say that your site visitor wants to find an environmentally friendly way of saving their lawn.

If you're a restaurant, your site visitor may want to check out your menu, see your hours, or get directions. They may also want to find a place to host a corporate event or a kid's birthday party.

Remember that this is about what **they** want, not what you want.

Who are your three biggest competitors?

Avoid the "No one. No one does what we do" answer here. Keep in mind that even if no one does exactly what you do, there may be other solutions to your potential customers' problems.

You may have the only archery range in town that has a birthday room, but there are certainly other activities parents can choose that will entertain a dozen ten-year-olds.

If you really find yourself struggling to find other businesses that are similar, consider businesses you don't compete with because of geography. You may be the first gluten-free bakery in your town, but there are plenty of others you can find across the country.

If you're doing something completely revolutionary, market ignorance could be your biggest competitor. In that case, education and content creation will be critical to your success.

How do you differentiate yourself from these competitors?

This will help guide your copy, the photos you choose, and all of your marketing. You should be crystal clear on what these differentiators are. Visit your competitors' sites (if appropriate) to understand how they are positioning themselves.

Your Website

If your website had a job description, what would it be?

Imagine you were hiring for this position...what would that job description look like?

- To educate parents on the dangers of lawn pesticides and show them there's a safer way that actually works.
- To generate leads from local small businesses who are too small to have an internal HR person but need help staying compliant with state laws.
- To sell home decor products from our online store.

What is the main reason you are redesigning your website?

Is your website tired looking? Is it not mobile-friendly? Is it not generating enough traffic or leads? Did you recently change your name or branding and now your website is out of sync with the rest of your marketing?

Are you introducing a new product? Looking to attract a new audience segment? Did you outgrow your neighbor's brother-in-law?

What is the main business problem you hope to solve with your new website?

Do you need more search engine visibility? Traffic? Leads? Are you launching a new product and you need to build awareness? Are you trying to provide more value to your members? Are you trying to double sales this year?

How will you measure its success?

What are the KPIs (key performance indicators) that will help you track if and when your site is successful? It could be revenue goals, the number of leads, or downloads at your site.

If you currently have a site, what specific areas of your site are successful? Why?

Are there parts of your site, like a resource center or blog, that are working well? Do you have an Ask the Expert form that gets a lot of traction? Are there features of your online store that people really like, such as a comparison tool or ability to zoom in on a product photo?

Which are unsuccessful? Why?

Don't fall into the "ugly baby" syndrome here. That's where you hear from people that they love your website. Nice to hear, but who ever told a parent they have an ugly baby? The same is true with an ugly or ineffective website. People don't tell you, they just leave.

One thing you can do is look at your Google Analytics (assuming you have it set up). It can help you identify underperforming pages. Pages where people visit but then leave your website.

Or perhaps you have a lot of shopping cart abandonment. Or people aren't signing up for your email newsletter. Or you hate the colors of your site. Or it's difficult to make updates. You get the picture.

Use a few adjectives to describe your brand's identity.

This isn't Mad Libs. Try and be as spot on with your brand (as you see it.) Are you irreverent or trustworthy? Cutting edge or established? Modern or traditional? Transparent or mysterious?

Use a few adjectives to describe how you'd like your site visitors to perceive your website.

There will hopefully be some overlap in vibe, if not in word, with the previous question. Professional. Modern. Fast-loading. Easy. Surprising. Deep. Clean. Organized. Fun.

From a design perspective, list three websites you like and why.

These don't need to be in your industry. The last thing you want is a me-too website that looks like a competitor's in a reversible jacket.

Why do you like them? Is it the photos? The structure? The navigation? The color scheme? A specific element on the site that makes it easier to use?

Do you have marketing material that the website must complement?

Marketing and branding are all about consistency. Your website should match your business cards should match your signage should match your slide deck, should match your...you get the idea.

Is your logo up-to-date and representative of your brand?

I bring this up because we've designed modern looking websites that almost fall apart because of a dated or poorly designed logo. It's like pairing a classic black tuxedo with a My Little Pony bowtie. (Not judging here.)

If time and budget aren't pressing concerns, have a professional assess your logo.

Do you have brand colors?

Some colors don't work as well online as they do IRL. See: yellow.

Also, just because a color appears in your logo doesn't mean it has to be part of your website palette. In fact, choosing different colors can help your logo pop and be more memorable for your site visitors.

Your Marketing

A lot of questions about your marketing have already been answered in the questions about your business and your website. However, these questions will help determine where you want to invest your marketing efforts.

How important is search visibility to your business?

While some people feel that the only purpose of their website is to give people a place to evaluate their business after a referral, most businesses will still benefit from a presence on the search engines. How important search is to you will help determine what type of investment you need to make.

According to a recent article from Infront Webworks [theleadmachinebook.com/infront] the top 10 results on the first page of a search get 91.5% of clicks, followed by 4.8%, 1.1%, and 0.4% respectively for each page that follows. Whether a lead is worth $10 to your business or $10,000, you can see the value of appearing on the first page for relevant searches. When trying to determine the budget for SEO, keep in mind the opportunity lost by not being on the first page.

In the chapter on SEO, we'll dig deeper into how you can reach the first page of search results for your targeted keywords.

Is your location important when it comes to search?

Google's local search results show a "snack pack" of three local providers.

These generally appear above the organic results. If your business is "geographically challenged," then getting into the snack pack can be critical to your success. There are a lot of factors that go into these results, from location to citations to reviews.

Again, we'll look at more factors that impact whether you get into the snack pack in the SEO section.

What are some of the keywords and keyphrases that your ideal customer would Google to find a company, product, or service like yours?

This is a great brainstorming exercise that gets you thinking about how your potential customers *really* search for you.

What are the 5-10 most common questions you get from customers?

Think of the questions you get every day from your customers. The questions about durability. The questions about how the product or service works. The questions about price. If you're not sure, ask your sales team. Your customer service reps. Re-read emails from customers. Check the intake forms on your website.

If these people knew enough to ask you, that's great! But think of the thousands who have the same question, but don't know who to ask. Who do they ask? They ask Google. And if your answer is one of the best results, Google will drive all those people to your site.

Where does your audience hang out online?

Maybe they hang out on Facebook. Or Pinterest. Maybe there's a Harley Davidson discussion forum where they spend most of their time. Or a forum for quilters. Maybe they like watching videos, or listening to podcasts, or reading the local paper online.

Wherever *they* hang out is where *you* need to hang out, too. And if it's not a place you can hang out, maybe you can write articles there, or advertise or sponsor the content.

If you're absolutely convinced they don't hang out online, you may need to consider more traditional methods to drive traffic to your site, such as TV ads, billboards, or the Pony Express.

If you're not sure where they hang out, consider sending a survey to your current customer base, asking them where they spend most of their online time. You can create a free survey using Survey Monkey [theleadmachinebook.com/surveymonkey] or Google Drive [theleadmachinebook.com/googledrive].

Recently, I recorded a podcast with Beth Hayden where she discussed some advanced tactics for finding out where your audience is online. You can listen to that show (or read the transcript) at theleadmachinebook.com/whereswaldo

How many hours a week does your business have to put towards digital marketing?

This will help you prioritize what you're going to focus on. There's a big difference between being able to spend an hour a week and 20 hours a week on your digital marketing. If you don't have much time, but need a lot of marketing, you may need to hire someone to write your content and promote it through social channels.

Do you like to write?

If so, writing blog posts, email newsletters, and white papers may be a great way to grow your business. If you hate writing, or you're not a great writer, consider outsourcing this or finding a different platform to build credibility.

Do you like to speak?

If you like to speak, podcasts, webinars, or online videos might be a good fit.

Is your product, service, or other offering "demonstrable?"
If so, videos might help drive interest, traffic, and sales.

Your Assets

For this section you're just trying to get a handle on everything you need when assembling your website. It's kind of like putting out all the ingredients before you start cooking.

Do you have photos to use on the website?
While stock photography can fill the gaps, you're not going to use stock photography for staff photos or the front of your building. Stock photos are an affordable solution, but they can be used by anyone, including your competitors. Using cheesy photos on your website (two business people shaking hands, or a group of well-diversified happy employees gathered around a computer terminal) can undermine the credibility of your business.

Do you have videos to use on the website?
In general, videos should be stored off site on YouTube or Vimeo, and then embedded in your website.

Do you have a copywriter on staff?
I cannot stress enough the importance of a copywriter. If you are not one by trade, employ one, hire a contractor, or use the one provided by your digital agency.

Do you have analytics for your current site?
Looking at how people are finding and using your current website can greatly improve the effectiveness of your new site.

For example, on a previous version of flyte's website, I had a separate page for every presentation topic I covered. I wanted to clean up the site and streamline it, so I planned to remove those pages and just list my featured topics on one page.

After reviewing my analytics, however, I saw that those individual pages were pulling in hundreds of new visitors a month to our site from the search engines. Needless to say, they were spared the axe.

What Now?

At this end of this process, you should be crystal clear on the following items:

- Who this website is for (your ideal customer)
- Where you can reach them
- What they are suffering from (problems, needs)
- How your website can help solve or address their problems

Once you know the answers to these questions, a lot of the other pieces will fall into place.

Organizing Your Website

The *Harry Potter* series was an incredibly creative piece of fiction. If you disagree, please feel free to substitute your own favorite fiction here instead.

Also, you're a muggle.

But the story was still delivered in black type on a white background. The pages were still numbered in sequential order. The books were printed on paper, not made of holly and phoenix feathers.

The creativity was not in the structure, but rather in the storytelling.

A business website should be incredibly easy to use. Remember that 99.99% of the time, your site visitor is on a website that is **not** yours. Therefore, anything you do that is too clever or unexpected or confusing might get your new visitor to click the back button, never to return again.

When we build a house, we start with an architectural drawing. We need to know where the bedroom goes, whether the pantry is connected to the kitchen, and if there's a stairwell to the basement. We want to make sure there's a good, intuitive flow.

A sitemap plays a similar role.

How to Organize Your Site

When organizing your website, there are two major considerations: audiences and offerings. These don't need to be mutually exclusive, and you can organize by either or both.

Audiences

One way to organize a site is by audience. Maybe you offer software for hearing impaired children. Your audience may include parents, teachers, and school comptrollers. In the real world, you might have very different conversations with these three audiences based on the needs of each.

This can be solved with a primary navigation of Who We Serve with secondary navigation for Parents, Teachers and School Comptrollers. Alternatively, you might have a home page slideshow that addresses each audience type and their needs. By clicking on the image that speaks to the individual visitor, you can drive them to an internal page that speaks to their concerns.

Offerings

Many of us have multiple products or services. Some people are going to search or navigate based on these offerings. You might organize everything under one primary navigation button or several, depending on how many products or services you have.

Your sitemap vs. your navigation

Your navigation features the most important pages on your website. A guided tour of recommended stops. If you're old enough, envision the TripTik Travel Planners that AAA used to provide where they would map out the best path for you to get where you wanted to go.

Your sitemap is a listing of *all* the pages of a website. It may display the natural hierarchy of pages and show how everything is organized. Envision the fold-out maps we all stuffed in our glove boxes before every car and phone came with a GPS.

As you're organizing your site, you should keep both in mind. Let's imagine we're developing a site for a local child care center. The navigation might include:

1. Home
2. Your First Visit
   a. Directions
   b. Paperwork
3. Child Care Services
   a. Infants
   b. Toddlers
   c. After-School Programs
4. About Us
   a. Mission
   b. Staff
   c. In the News
4. Blog
5. Contact

The sitemap may include additional pages such as a Privacy Statement, Hours, and Testimonials that the site owner decided not to put on the main navigation. However, the sitemap probably wouldn't include every blog post the center ever wrote.

Every bullet point in the navigation and every page listed in the sitemap is, in fact, a webpage, and therefore needs content. For example, point 4., About Us, requires some content outside of just Mission, Staff, and In The News. It can be a glorified table of contents if you wish, but I'd still recommend putting some unique content on that About page. The blog home page will automatically pull snippets from the most recent blog posts, but it still requires that content.

Website Essentials

There are certain things that every business website needs. In this chapter I want to talk about a few of those things that you just can't do without.

Content Management System (CMS)

One of the biggest complaints new prospects have about their current website when they come to me is that they don't have enough—or any—control over their website. Early CMSs had their problems: they were bloated with code (making them slow-loading), weren't good for SEO, and the templates were so generic looking they could be spotted a mile away.

All of that has changed.

As more companies (and developers) have turned to CMS platforms, they have become lean, mean, lead generating machines. The best ones out there are fast-loading, come with plenty of SEO options, and can be customized an infinite number of ways.

There is no excuse not to be on a CMS.

Personally, I'm a big fan of WordPress. It's the world's most popular CMS by far and it's open source, meaning you're not tied to just one developer or agency. Drupal and Joomla are other popular open-source CMS platforms.

If you prefer a platform that's backed by a company, Square-Space and Wix are popular choices. They both come with monthly fees, but these may be less than what you would pay for a WordPress developer or agency if you needed to hire one.

The bottom line is there's no future-proofing your platform. I've seen platforms and programming languages come and go over the years. If you choose WordPress or SquareSpace, I can't guarantee either will be around in five years, but they're both safe bets.

One choice I'd be a little more concerned about is a home-grown platform from a small or medium-sized agency. Once you're on their platform, you're stuck with it, and with them.

Sometimes relationships with agencies sour. There's too much turnover, or they're constantly late on deliverables, or they get too big for you, or you get too big for them. It doesn't matter: you can't leave. Or at least, if you do leave, you're going to have to completely rebuild your website on another platform.

Unless there is some specific thing that this agency offers that you can't find at any other agency, the risk outstrips the reward.

Mobile-Friendly

More than half the world's internet traffic is delivered onto mobile devices these days. Admittedly, that's truer outside the US, where not everyone has a computer at work and another at home. But even in the US, mobile internet usage is growing rapidly.

While your site traffic may still be heavily reliant on desktop computers, there's no reason to exclude a significant portion of your site visitors. At this writing, 70% of our website traffic is from desktop computers. Could you imagine a store that turned away 30% of its potential customers?

Of course not.

Mobile devices are everywhere (um, almost by definition). People use them in line, at lunch, and in the bathroom. (One big reason to never ask to borrow someone's phone.)

Maybe they see your Facebook post. Or find you on Yelp. Or search for "dentist near me" and Google or Siri shows them your site as a result. If it's not mobile-friendly, they'll click the back button.

Through search, social, and digital ads, you'll be sending people on their phones to your website. If it's not mobile-friendly, you've lost that customer, probably forever.

While there are many ways to develop a mobile-friendly website, the most popular one (and the one that is currently most future-proof in my opinion) is called Responsive Web Design, or RWD.

One additional feature I recommend is a popup window that only appears on the mobile device that provides quick links to the items your mobile-visitor is most interested in. These may be Directions, Hours, or Contact.

Contact

Have you ever visited a website and struggled to find a way to contact the company behind it?

Infuriating, right?

If you want to get the phone ringing, you need to put your phone number at the top of each page. It's also important to make sure it's actually HTML text, not an image. That's because if it's text, your smartphone visitors can click it and call you. (That's right, your smartphone can double as a phone!)

If you want people emailing you, you need to have a contact form that collects information and sends it to you. I don't recommend having an email link, and here's why:

There are email scraping programs that grab all the email addresses off a website and deliver them to spammers and hackers. Even if your email doesn't appear on the page, but still appears in the website code, these programs can steal them. The best solution is using a contact form that doesn't include your email address at all.

I've heard some pushback over the years: it's too much to ask people to complete the online forms, forms feel impersonal, I hate filling out all that information on other people's forms, so why should I ask them to use mine?

In my opinion, if they're not willing to complete a short form on your website, they're probably not a qualified lead. In other words, it filters out the tire-kickers.

Second, you can collect a lot of great data people wouldn't think of providing in an email...everything from how they heard of you, to the company they work for, to their name!

Third, you don't have to ask for a ton of information. I only require the minimum amount of information I need to follow up with someone: their name, email, and phone. (I ask for their phone because often emails get caught in overly-aggressive spam filters, so if I haven't heard back in a couple of days, I can call them.)

Fourth, most forms can auto-populate your CRM, meaning you don't have to enter all that information in yourself. In fact, many can automatically add people to your email list...with their permission, naturally.

Last thought on forms: don't use a CAPTCHA. CAPTCHAs are those nearly impossible to read alpha-numeric combinations that you need to type in to submit a form. There are better tools out there to prevent someone (or some bot) from spamming your contact form. On WordPress, we are currently using the GravityForms plugin with great success.

NAP

Who doesn't love a good nap? In this case, it stands for Name, Address, and Phone. If your physical address is important to your business, having your NAP information on your site is essential. For everyone else, you can downgrade it to critical.

Any business that serves a geographic location—even if it's not the only audience you serve—needs NAP. That includes everyone from a donut shop to a B&B to a carpet cleaning company.

This NAP information is going to be shared with a number of online services, and it must be consistent across all sites. By consistent I mean that if you publish it as Elm St. in one place, that's how you need to publish it everywhere.

Not Elm St

Not Elm ST

Not Elm Street

Inconsistencies lead to duplicate entries that can hurt your visibility in local searches.

We'll talk about Local SEO in the SEO section.

Blog

Yes, I consider this critical to your website's success. A blog offers so many benefits:

- SEO
- An opportunity to brand yourself as an expert
- An easy way to publish fresh content
- A way to add pages without constantly updating your navigation

If you're really concerned about having a "blog" and keeping it fresh, call it something less intimidating, like "News & Events" or "Articles."

Calls to Action

Once someone is on your site, it may seem obvious what you want them to do. To call you, to book a room, or to buy now.

It's going to be less obvious to them. Especially if they don't know your company or what's typical in your industry.

They're looking for guidance. They're looking for an expert to make it easy for them and show them the way.

Calls to action help guide your site visitor's progress through the site. At the bottom of every page, you should tell them what you would like them to do next.

Call us today for a free estimate!

Download our eBook on 101 Ways to Save Money for College!

Join our mailing list and get 25% off your first order!

Calls to action help funnel people to the next logical step in the sales process. Often, these CTAs are links to other pages, buttons that open modal (popup) windows, or forms where people can contact you or sign up for your mailing list.

In other words, they can be interactive.

Opt-Ins

On my "Agents of Change" podcast, I interview digital marketing experts from around the world. Some are Facebook specialists, others are Twitter gurus, still others are experts on Pinterest, SEO, Instagram, etc.

Regardless of the platform, they all focus on one major, measurable tactic to grow their business: building their email list.

As sexy as social media is, and as important as SEO is, email marketing and list building are critical to your small business's online success. I'll go into more detail when we get to email marketing, but for now, you should plan on including ways in which you can get people to opt into your mailing list.

You may feel that we covered this in the CTA section, but building your own list is so important I wanted to break it out into its own section.

Plan on having multiple places where you ask for people's emails and try different incentives to get them on your list. Again, we'll go into greater detail in the email marketing section.

Security

While your site visitors won't see the security on your site, they might see it if you don't take security seriously.

Over the years, I've spoken with many website owners that woke up one day to find that their website had disappeared, was defaced, or that site visitors received a popup that warned them that the site wasn't safe and to "proceed at your own risk."

Think any new prospects will roll the dice on that one?

The more popular a CMS platform, the bigger a target it becomes for hackers and spammers. The best thing you can do for security's sake is make sure that:

- You're running the most up to date version of the software (which includes the latest security patches)
- You're making regular backups of your site (hosting companies will do this, but often overwrite one daily backup with another, meaning that unless you catch a hacker within 24 hours, they're overwriting a good file with an infected version)
- You've installed some additional plugins that include firewalls and other protection against hacks.

Will this guarantee you never get hacked? No, but it will make you a much less attractive target.

Analytics

How will you know how effective your website is if you don't have a way to measure it?

For most small businesses, the best solution to getting great insights into your site traffic is Google Analytics. It's free, it's powerful, and it can provide you with critical information on how to improve your website and your digital marketing.

If you are working with an agency, it's important that they use *your* Google Analytics account rather than setting you up under their own. If you don't have an account yet, you can add one to your Google account for free. If you don't have that, you can create a new Google account which comes with Gmail and gives you the ability to set up Analytics, too.

I recommend that you have a dedicated Google account for your business. This is helpful because if you tie it to an employee's Google account and they leave, you won't lose access to all that important information.

Wrapping Up

These are the elements that every small business website needs. However, it's not *everything* your website may need. In the next chapter, we'll look at a few popular features that might help your business grow more quickly.

Other Important Elements

Over the past 20 years, we've worked with a wide variety of clients, businesses, and industries. Each has certain requirements that can be addressed with the right tool. While not all of these elements are critical to every business, some may improve your conversion rate.

Search

Some people may consider a search box an essential tool on your site. For larger sites or big e-commerce sites, this may be true. But for a small site of under twenty or twenty-five pages, a search box might just clutter up your site.

Remember that every element you add to your site reduces the importance of every other element. Unless something serves a purpose and helps you accomplish your business goals, you should get rid of it.

Most CMS platforms come with built in search boxes, as well as plugins that may have more features and flexibility. You can also choose to go with a third party search box like the one that Google offers.

Calendar

If you have a lot of events that you want to share, an online calendar can be a great way to promote them.

If you only have one or two events a month, I would recommend that you just list your events. Showing a monthly calendar that's almost empty is overkill, and makes it look like you don't have a lot going on.

If you have several events a week, then you should look at a calendar plugin like Events Manager Pro [theleadmachinebook.com/calendar]. I recommend that you have the name of the event in the calendar, but make it clickable so people can get more information—or even register—at your site.

If you have multiple events a day, your calendar should be able to show all events, but also filter by type of event. For example, we built a calendar page for a hospital that wanted to list all of their departments' events. That was often several per day. By choosing a category like Cardiology or Women's Health, only events tagged as such would appear in the calendar view.

Slideshow

Slideshows appear most often on the home page, where multiple images rotate through a billboard-like space. Slideshows are powerful because they can quickly give site visitors a better idea of what you offer in a limited space. They allow the visitor to self-select, and then take them deeper within the site.

The best slideshows include the ability for site visitors to pause, choose, or rotate through the slides. They also include the ability for you, as the site owner, to add or edit text that overlays the images so you don't have to go back to a designer every time you want to tweak the message. They should also be clickable, sending visitors to important pages within your site.

While there's no limit to the number of slides you can use, I generally recommend three to five. Any less than three and I wonder why you needed the slideshow in the first place, and any more than five and you will significantly slow down the page load time.

Scheduler

I love jumping on my favorite massage therapist's website and booking a time. That's what I call frictionless. I can make the appointment anytime from anywhere and know it's locked in for me.

One of our clients is a canine behavior specialist who offers individual coaching as well as group classes. She has a scheduler that can handle either and cuts off registrations to the class once it fills up.

If you run an appointment-based business, including a scheduler app on your site can increase appointments and cut down on staff time with back and forth emails to find a time that works for everyone.

I have talked to some businesses that don't want a scheduler. One dentist's office decided against it as they already had too many no-shows and they didn't want to add to the pile. Others only want it for current clients, and require new people to speak to them by phone or in person.

You should ultimately decide what's best for your business.

E-Commerce

Not every business needs e-commerce. Many businesses only need their website to generate leads. Even those that need to be able to sell online have choices outside their website. Amazon, Etsy, eBay and Shopify are just a few of the offerings you can use independent of your main site.

However, if you want to keep your visitors onsite, having an order form or shopping cart is the way to go. Just keep in mind that there are a lot of moving parts to an e-commerce site:

- Special, PCI (Payment Card Industry) compliant hosting
- Security certificate
- Merchant account
- Shopping cart software
- Shipping and fulfillment considerations

And a whole lot more. A deep dive into e-commerce is a little outside the scope of this book, but there are plenty of books, conferences, and online resources for those looking to set up shop online.

Ticket Sales

Putting on events? You'll probably want to sell tickets.

My favorite tool is EventBrite [theleadmachinebook.com/eventbrite], and we've used it for all of our Agents of Change conferences, as well as most of the workshops we put on. It's free to use, but they will add a surcharge if you're collecting fees for your tickets. You can, however, pass those fees along to your attendees.

EventBrite has a widget that can embed into your site, making it easy to collect registration information and money for your events.

I'm sure there are plenty of other great tools out there, but EventBrite is our go-to ticket registration service.

MLS

Short for multi-listing service, this is what powers real estate websites, many car dealerships, and used boat sites as well. The information is provided from a third party service and you can embed this information into your website in a number of ways.

Other Tools

As you can see, there are a number of enhancements you can add to your website. These might come as plugins for your CMS, a widget from a third party service, or a custom programming job from a developer.

Just remember that your website doesn't need to be all things to all people. I'm a big fan of starting small and nimble, and adding features as needed.

When do I optimize my site for the search engines?

The best time to optimize your site for the search engines is before you build it. That's not to say that you can't optimize a website that's already been built, just that it's more work that way. It's sort of like deciding you need a bathroom in the basement; it's a lot easier and cheaper when the house is still an architect's blueprint, rather than when you've already put all the furniture in the living room.

The keyword research—an early step in SEO—might change your navigation, and it's definitely going to require writing or rewriting your website copy.

If you need SEO, you may want to skip ahead to that section and then come back here.

It's OK, go ahead. I'll wait. Actually, I'll meet you in the next chapter.

Writing Your Copy

Whether you've done your keyword research (part of your SEO) or not, you want to make sure you're writing the best, most persuasive copy possible. Even if SEO isn't your main concern, it's important to understand what the search engines are looking for, because it's often the same things your ideal customers are looking for.

In *The Lead Machine Workbook*, you'll find a sample Content Intake Packet that you can use. That's a document that will help you populate the different pages of your website.

Before you get started, I wanted to share a popular post from the flyte blog entitled:

The 11 Commandments of Creating Compelling Web Copy for the Non-Copywriter

Whether you're creating your first website or revamping your current site, the most critical piece is the copy. It's also the most time consuming, difficult, and frustrating for the average small business owner.

Good web copy is search engine friendly, easy to read or scan, and persuades your visitor to take action. If you've never written copy specifically for the web, we've put together some tips to help your copy be all it can be.

What follows are the 11 Commandments for Writing Copy for the Non-Copywriter.

I. Hire a copywriter.

I know—these are the 11 Commandments for the do-it-your-selfer. So why am I bothering to tell you to hire a copywriter?

I hear it all the time from business owners we work with:

- No one knows my business like I do.
- I don't want to spend the money on a copywriter because I know how to write.
- The copy will write itself.

Let's look at your objections one at a time.

Yes, it's true no one knows your business like you do, and that may be the problem. You may need someone from outside your industry to translate your offerings into benefits your ideal customer can understand.

Yes, you know how to write. Doubtless you've written thousands of emails, hundreds of proposals and possibly a book or two. But copywriting is a completely different skill, and uses a completely different set of mental muscles.

Copywriting is all about being persuasive. Getting someone to take a desired action at your website.

U.S.A. Track and Field would never put their top sprinter in the marathon with hopes of a winning gold medal. It's a completely different type of race. The same is true of writing copy.

Copywriters are professionals. They know just which words to use to invoke emotions. To identify problems. To clarify needs. To get someone to make a buying decision on your website.

No, the copy won't write itself. If you have a 10 to 12-page website that needs writing, expect to spend 30-40 hours on that project. That's a full working week where you won't be making any sales calls. Writing any proposals. Putting out any fires. Paying any bills. Running your business.

You're basically going to take a week's vacation to write the copy on your site.

If you hire a copywriter, you not only get that week back, you know that the copy is to going to be written on time, on budget, and will be professionally crafted to get your site visitor to take a desired action.

And if you hire the right copywriter, she can optimize your content for the search engines. Do you know enough about SEO to make that happen?

Not only that, that copy will continue to attract visitors, market your business, and generate leads for years to come.

II. Keep the focus on your visitors.

Too many websites have "About Us" content on the home page. Let me be blunt:

No one cares about you or your business. (At least not at first.)

They don't care about your mission statement, your customer service philosophy, how long you've been in business...not even about your products and services! They only care about one thing: themselves.

As the old adage goes, everyone's tuned into the same radio station: WII-FM. (What's In It For Me?)

Your visitors are at your website because they have a need or a problem. Talk first about *their* problems, *their* needs, *their* situation. After you've addressed these issues, *then* you can talk about how you can help.

Take this test: after you've written the home page copy count up the number of times you use "we" words: we, us, our, or your company name, and compare it to the number of times you use "you" words: you, your, etc. The "you's" should have it.

III. Write to one person.

Although thousands (if not millions!) of visitors will come to your home page, they'll be filing in one-at-a-time. Don't try to talk to all of them...instead talk to *each* of them.

Imagine you're having a one-on-one conversation with your best prospect or customer and write as you'd talk to her. The people who are most like your best prospect will respond to this message—these are the people most likely to buy, subscribe, or join.

IV. Start every web page with a descriptive page title.

You're actually writing for at least two audiences: people and search engines. And although search engines will never buy your products or services, they can deliver qualified traffic to your website.

To get the search engines to deliver your ideal customer to your site, you'll need to know and use the appropriate keywords that your prospects are using when they search.

How do you know what your effective keywords should be? How can you determine which words will drive qualified traffic to your website and compel people to take action?

You can either guess at what your prospects are searching for, or you can run a Keyword Analysis. A Keyword Analysis will uncover the most effective keywords based on actual search engine results and competition in your niche.

Once you've uncovered the best keywords for you, start by using them in your page titles. Start with descriptive page titles that explain succinctly and specifically what the focus of the page is. Don't use a generic phrase like "Services" when you can title a page "Holistic Healing in Portland, Maine," "Consulting for Family Owned Businesses," or whatever is appropriate for you.

Your page title is the "big blue link" on the search engine results page, so it's often the first impression prospects have of your business. Make sure this title gives people a compelling reason to click on your link and not the link of your competition.

Make sure that every page gets a unique page title that tells your prospect what they can expect.

V. Support descriptive titles with complementary headers and copy.

It's not enough to have a compelling, keyword rich title. The rest of your copy needs to deliver on the promise of your title.

It's usually considered best practice to work your targeted keyword phrase into the first sentence or two. It should also appear in any headers or subheaders as appropriate. Search engines may read every word on your page, but people tend to scan. By using headers and subheaders to break up the page into natural sections, you allow your visitors to quickly find the information that's most valuable to them.

By using the right keywords effectively throughout your pages, you'll rank higher at the search engines for those phrases...all other things being equal.

VI. Use your keywords in your anchor text.

Anchor text refers to the words that are "hyperlinked" to another page. These words are often underlined and appear in a different color from the rest of the text. Search engines consider these words more important than non-linked words and phrases.

How can you take advantage of this? Instead of creating a link from your home page to your resources page that says "Resources," be specific: "Public Speaking Resources," "Resources for Home Schooling," or "Resources for People Suffering from ADHD."

Search engines will now have a better idea of what the linked-to web page is all about and should rank it higher...again, all other things being equal.

And whatever you do, don't use "Click here" or "Learn more" if you're looking to help your visitors or the search engines out. That's just a missed opportunity.

In addition, the descriptive hyperlink is more helpful to your site visitors.

VII. Narrow the focus of each page.

Search engines prefer specialists over generalists. The search engine results page is Darwinism in action.

Search engines want to provide users with web pages that are most likely to answer their search query. Therefore, the tighter the focus of your page, the more likely it is to answer a specific question.

While it's true that a narrower focus means the page will come up for fewer searches, your goal is to bring qualified traffic, not just anyone, to your website. Concentrate on the people you are most likely to help.

Your site visitors will appreciate you not wasting their time.

VIII. Keep your copy short and easy-to-read.

Reading words on a web page is difficult. Eyestrain, short-attention spans and our desire for instant gratification all dictate shortened copy.

Use as few words as possible to get your point across. While some search engine experts say that every page should have 300 – 500 words minimum (for search engine optimization purposes), it's most important to use what's right for you and your audience.

If you have longer copy, break up paragraphs into smaller pieces...use headers and sub-headers to give readers an idea of what's coming and what they may be able to skip over. (Note the big subheaders in this article.)

If your paragraphs still look like dense blocks of text, use extra paragraph breaks, **bold** and *italicized* text to stress important ideas—dashes and ellipses as well...they all break up paragraphs nicely. And everyone loves a bulleted list.

Important Note: Never use underlines on the web for emphasis...they are reserved for links only. You'll frustrate visitors who will click on underlined words.

IX. Be specific.

Vague, superlative words have little impact on your prospect. People tune out words like "greatness," "excellence," and "quality." To counter this, give a specific example that helps your visitor visualize the value of your offering.

As copywriter Jonathan Kranz wrote, "If you want to scare the cloak off Little Red Riding Hood, don't lecture her about the woods and its perils—put the wolf's hot breath on her neck."

What about your product or service has the impact of the wolf's hot breath?

X. Create calls-to-action.

Buy now. Subscribe to our newsletter. Complete this form. Enter our sweepstakes.

This isn't a creative writing class. The purpose of copy is to sell... to sell your product, your service or your idea.

You need to ask for the "sale" at least once on each page. Don't assume your site visitors know what's expected of them. At the bottom of every page, there should be a call-to-action. What that call-to-action is depends entirely on your business and website goals.

Don't forget to ask for that sale. For example...

- "Download our free report on carcinogens in your home."
- "Enter our drawing for a free iPod."
- "Sign our petition to stop late fees at the library."

XI. Hire a copywriter.

Yeah, this again.

If you're serious about increasing your online visibility, driving more qualified traffic to your site and converting more of that traffic into leads and sales, you'll hire a copywriter.

Surely, your time can be better spent doing something else, like running your business...right?

****

As I re-read that post, my big takeaways include:

- Your website is not about you, it's about your site visitor.
- People don't read, they skim. Write for skimmers.
- Don't assume people know what to do. Guide them with calls to action at the bottom of every page.

And one thing I didn't include:

- Every page is a landing page.

What I mean by that is that *any* page on your website could be the first your site visitor sees. Maybe they find your services page first through Google, or enter your site through your blog post because of something a friend shared on Facebook, or land on a store product page because of an ad.

This means that every page, and every blog post, deserves a compelling title, easy-to-read copy, one or more engaging images, and a strong call to action.

Some final thoughts on writing your copy:

- Doing your keyword research is important even if you don't think the search engines are going to deliver you traffic. Consider it market research into what words your ideal customer is using.
- Write to one person...your ideal customer.
- Break up your copy with headers and subheaders, short paragraphs, lists, and as much white space as makes sense.
- Guide your visitor through the process with strong calls to action.

How to Increase Conversions

Imagine trying to fill a colander with water. No matter how much water you pour in, no matter how strong the water pressure is, it doesn't matter. Water comes in, and water goes out just as quickly.

In the next section we'll talk about the art of Attraction and driving more people to your site. However, if your website isn't set up to convert traffic into leads, it doesn't matter how many visitors you get...you'll be like that colander, leaking just as much traffic as you attract.

Build Trust Immediately

Years ago, a plastic surgeon hired us to increase his search visibility and traffic. He didn't want us to change anything on the site, just improve his SEO. The only thing he would allow us to change were the title tags and converting his image-based navigation to text.

I was less experienced then, so I agreed to having our hands tied when it came to helping him.

Six months later he emailed me, very upset. He said he had paid us to optimize his site, but he wasn't getting any more traffic than he had before.

This was in the early days of Google Analytics, so before I called him back, I checked his analytics. It turns out those little changes we made had increased his search traffic by an astounding 600%!

However, the problem was that almost all of his traffic, a whopping 95%, left within 10 seconds of arriving at his site. They came, they saw, they were disappointed. So they left.

The site didn't have a lot of copy, so it had no way to address the questions and concerns of the potential patient. Nor did it explain why you should choose this particular doctor. The copy it did have wasn't persuasive.

The site had very little photography. No pictures that showed how clean and welcoming his office was. One tiny picture of him and no picture of his staff. You had no idea if his office was in the nicest building in town or a run-down warehouse by the railroad tracks. It did have a few questionable before and after photos, as all cosmetic surgeon sites are "required" to, but these were poorly lit and the "after" pictures were taken just days after surgery, when the scars were still fresh.

Pro tip for plastic surgeons: "After" photos should be taken at least six months after the surgery, when people look their best.

And although beauty is subjective, this site was ugly. In an objective, *I-think-we-can-all-agree-on-this-one* sort of way.

If you're going to ask people to spend thousands or tens of thousands of dollars on elective surgery to make themselves look beautiful, you need to prove to them that you understand what beauty is!

In short, the site didn't build trust with the site visitors, so they went elsewhere.

If you want to increase conversions, you need to build trust right out of the gate.

Making a Good First Impression

Before I started flyte new media, I was a traveling salesman. I spent a lot of time going from nursing home to nursing home, selling medical products. I ate out a lot. Often I chose McDonald's because I was 25 years younger, nothing I ate would put weight on me, and I hadn't seen the movie *Supersize Me* yet.

But in certain towns there was no McDonald's, or I had just eaten there the day before, or I had eaten there for breakfast. In those cases, I needed to choose a place to eat that I had never heard of before. (As you can imagine, this was eons before apps like Yelp.)

So how did I decide? First impressions.

Was it in a safe neighborhood? Did the place appear clean? How was the signage?

Honestly, I probably chose more unknown restaurants based on the signage alone. I figured, if they spent enough money to have a really kickass sign, they probably took pride in what they made, even if it was just sandwiches.

And you know what? A good sign rarely steered me wrong.

When people arrive at your website, they are going to make a snap decision on whether or not to trust you.

They're going to make this decision before they read your content. Before they click through to a second page. And definitely before they sign up for your email newsletter.

The photos, the colors, and the layout of the page will send subconscious messages to your site visitors on whether they should trust or distrust you. Whether they should stick around or flee.

One thing to keep in mind is that not all first impressions should be the same. The first impression for a toy store should be markedly different than that of an august law firm. If you switched the branding of these two companies, they'd both fail.

Making a good first impression means showing off your best side, not pretending to be something that you are not. If I want a greasy spoon diner experience, I won't be happy if I show up and the place looks like an upscale restaurant with cloth napkins and white linen service.

Making a Good First Impression from Search

Some of your traffic will come from the search engines. In this case, the first impression they'll have of your business is the big, blue link on the search engine results page, as well as the descriptive text below.

To make a good first impression here, don't just cram all your keywords in the title (which appears as the big blue link.) Think about what you might what to say to get a potential customer's attention without turning them off.

The black text below comes from your meta-description (more often than not). This is an opportunity to say a little more about your company or the topic at hand, and to reinforce the idea that you are a trusted resource and worthy of their click.

Making a Good First Impression from Social

Some social media sites allow you a certain amount of visual branding in your profile. Facebook, Twitter, and YouTube are obvious examples, but almost all sites allow you to customize and choose your avatar or profile picture.

If you can include a custom header image, try and make it complementary or identical to the header image on your website's home page. That way, if they travel from your Facebook page to your website to check you out, there's not a visual disconnect when they get there.

Making a Good First Impression from Mobile

Make sure you have a mobile-friendly website. If visitors arrive at your site and they have to pinch, zoom, stretch, double-tap...

in other words, if they have to treat your website like a ball of dough, then it's not mobile-friendly.

Now I have heard from some business owners that they actually prefer *that* experience over what the rest of us refer to as mobile-friendly. While everyone is entitled to their opinion, keep in mind that the vast majority of your site visitors won't appreciate that. And your website isn't about you, it's about your site visitors.

Also, you're disagreeing with Google. And Google has made it abundantly clear that they are going to be penalizing sites that aren't mobile-friendly. So, if your preference for a non-mobile friendly website outweighs your customers' desires and Google driving traffic to your site, then by all means....

It may seem unfair that people will judge us before they even read our content—that they'll judge us first by our looks and not by our brains—but that's human nature. To increase conversions, you'll need to be firing on all cylinders: you'll need to have a good-looking site and valuable content.

Social Proof

Have you ever tried that social experiment where you get a bunch of people to all look up? Suddenly everyone around them is looking up, even if they don't know why.

We visit review sites, ask friends, and form a queue even when we're not 100% sure that we're really in line to get into the concert. This is in part because we don't have time to assess every situation, so we look to other people to get clues on what's valuable and what's not.

Sometimes visitors come to our site already holding social proof, because they were referred by a friend. But for everyone else, we need to prove that we're the right choice, and to do it as quickly as possible.

Testimonials

One way to show social proof is to show people who have used your product or service and gotten good results from it.

When it comes to displaying testimonials at your site, the more you can do to tie a positive sentiment to a real person, the better. This is because your site visitor may not know you from Adam. Or Eve. So if you have a nice quote from "A. Smith," or worse, "a doctor," it won't mean as much as having that person's full name and city attached. That additional information makes it feel more real. Sure, you could have made up all that information, but since someone could more easily track down Alex Smith from Cooperstown, NY, to ask if he really said that, there's added legitimacy to the quote.

It can also be beneficial if this person is well known in your industry or city. Years ago, when I first discovered Derek Halpern's SocialTriggers.com website, I had no idea who he was. But in the top banner, next to the email signup box was a quote from Chris Brogan: "I'm totally digging Social Triggers!"

Chris is a respected leader in our industry, and I figured if he liked this site, so would I. Needless to say, I signed up.

Even more powerful than a written testimonial is a video testimonial. If you have an actual customer talking to the viewer, telling her how much better their business, life, or marriage is after working with you, that's incredibly persuasive.

One final word about website testimonials: no one ever wants to go read an entire page of testimonials. Instead, sprinkle them throughout the site. A quote here, another quote there. It's especially powerful if you offer different services and the quotes are relevant to the content on that page.

Social Shares

Another way you can show off social proof is through social sharing buttons. You'll find these at the top of most blog posts and product pages. Many—if not most—of these buttons include share counts, which will give your site visitor an immediate indication of whether other people thought your post or product was valuable.

Blog Comments

This is another way to learn if people are engaged with your content. If people are leaving comments, it means that they had a strong reaction to your post and wanted to weigh in. (Or, they were just trying to increase their own visibility and hijack some of your traffic, but let's ignore that for now.)

Audience Size

Recently I visited the website of Basecamp, a project management software we use. On the right column was a free trial signup that announced:

> Just last week, 7,586 companies got started with Basecamp 3!

I mean, if over 7,500 companies just got started with this software last week, it must be good, right? It's encouraging that so many other companies are taking the plunge. It reduces the apparent risk in trying the product out.

Similarly, I've seen websites share how many people are on their mailing list as a reason to subscribe: "Join 10,000/20,000/50,000 other marketers/authors/bail bondsmen (bondspersons?) who get critical information delivered right to their inbox each week!" Whether these numbers are real or not is almost beside the point: social proof is being built.

While not all site visitors will rely on social proof to make a buying decision, showing that your product or service worked for other, similar people can provide you with the benefit of the doubt.

Using Authority Sites

Similar to the celebrity endorsement mentioned above, many site owners like showing off a bunch of shiny, authoritative logos.

Small businesses might include the BBB (Better Business Bureau), a local chamber of commerce, or badge from an industry certification board.

A speaker or consultant might include places they've been interviewed or quoted, like CNN, *the Wall Street Journal,* or *Inc. Magazine.*

While I believe that Authority Buttons mean more to the site owner than to the visitor, for the educated prospect, they can alleviate worries about risk and increase the chances someone choosing you. However, they're much more valuable when your audience is familiar with the brand or certification. I once worked with a plastic surgeon (not the same one) who was adamant that we show off his board certification. I asked, "Don't all cosmetic surgeons have to be board certified?" Apparently they don't, but for me, as a lay person, that meant nothing as I would assume that all surgeons are board certified.

You may be inclined to link offsite to the certifying bodies.

Don't.

All that does is take the site visitor—who you've worked so hard to get—and send them away, likely never to return again. What value are you providing to your visitor if you link to that certifying site? To throw them into a site that might link back out to you...and all of your competitors?

If your visitor is so interested in finding out more about The Association of Michigan-Based Naturopaths, then let her Google it!

Site Speed

Site speed, or how fast your site loads, is becoming more critical as time goes on. First, if a visitor has to wait too long for a page to load, they'll become frustrated and hit the back button. There's no chance at conversion if your visitor isn't going to wait long enough for your Buy Now button to load.

Second, site speed impacts your search visibility. Google has been tracking site speed statistics for years and has confirmed that it is a factor in how your site is ranked. In your Google Analytics, there's even a report on site speed, along with suggestions on how to make your pages load faster.

Faster loading sites mean more conversions.

Simplify

Site owners unnecessarily complicate their sites. Too many buttons. Too many moving images. Too many fonts. Too many colors. Too many offers.

Or they accidentally hide the information visitors want most, whether it's hours, directions, pricing, or a way to contact the site owner.

Or they get too clever with what they name things, leading to a *What's Behind Link #2* feeling for their site visitors.

In short, they add unneeded complication to their websites, confusing their visitors.

All of these things are points of friction. Friction slows down conversion. See what you can do to remove any friction from your website.

For most small businesses, it doesn't matter how many pages a visitor looks at, or how much time they spend on your site. It only matters if they sign up for your email newsletter, fill out your contact form, or pick up the phone.

Photos

Another way to guide visitors to take a desired action is by purposeful use of photography. Human beings are wired to look at faces, but also to look where people are looking...to see what holds *their* attention.

In a fascinating eye-tracking study, James Breeze, a usability specialist, compared two diaper ads. The first one had a baby looking straight out while the second one turned the baby towards the advertising copy. The difference was astounding! People spent much more time looking at the ad copy and the logo in the second ad.

As Breeze states, "You look where they look."

You can use this knowledge to help guide people around your website. If you're using photos (or illustrations) of people on your site, they should be facing towards the page, not away from it. They should be looking at action items, such as signups and links, to direct the visitor's attention towards what you want her to focus on.

Action Color

In the early days of the web, unvisited links were blue and underlined, and visited links were purple and underlined. It was simple and straightforward.

But as talented print designers with backgrounds in branding came to the scene, they demanded more choice. Soon, any color could represent a visited or unvisited link, underlines were optional, **bolding** a link was a possibility, and even just rolling over a link might create an action (changing its color, changing the background behind it, or underlining it, for example.)

While this may be good for an individual company's branding, it has made navigating different websites more confusing. Is a bold phrase a link, or is the site just adding emphasis? Does a purple word mean the page has already been visited, or is that just their company color scheme?

Therefore, colors can play an important role in guiding visitors and helping them navigate what may be unfamiliar territory.

I recommend choosing **one** Action Color for your website. This is a color that will be used for links, buttons, and all calls to action. It should be reserved for these desired activities. In other words, don't make your headers and your action color the same.

There's only one red X that marks the spot on a treasure map, and your color scheme should be similar.

Limit Choices

In one of my favorite pieces of research, a team led by psychologists Sheena Iyengar and Mark Lepper, set up a tasting station at an upscale grocery store. At one point, they put out six flavors of jam. Later, they put out twenty-four flavors of jam. The bigger display, with more choices, attracted more people.

However, when it came to making a purchase, those who saw the bigger display were only *one tenth* as likely to buy jam as the group who saw the smaller display.

It's as if they were overwhelmed by the number of "wrong choices" they could make and so made no choice at all.

And it was jam! There is no wrong choice with jam!

This phenomenon is often referred to as the paradox of choice. Sure, people say they want choice, but what they really want is guidance.

This idea is incredibly important when it comes to your website. If you offer too many choices, more site visitors will choose the back button.

Choices on websites come in many flavors. You might have too many links. Too many photos in your slideshow. Too many buttons. Too many offers.

While certain sites, like Amazon, Target, or Home Depot, might benefit from having a nearly unlimited amount of choices, these are known brands. For most small businesses, it's important to simplify the decision-making and buying process.

If you have a lot of products or services to offer, try following the rule of threes. Divvy up your offerings into three distinct categories. Once your visitor chooses a category, show them another three choices, and so on.

There's another idea, popularized in the book *Nudge: Improving Decisions About Health, Wealth, and Happiness*, by Richard H. Thaler and Cass R. Sunstein. It's that we can help people make the right decisions **and** offer choices by having a default or recommended choice.

One great example of this is when software as a service companies offer different tiers of service. Basecamp used to offer three tiers with the benefits and prices of each listed in columns on their web page.

The middle tier, called Plus, was in a wider, center column and was labeled their "Most Popular Plan." In no small part, I'm sure, because it was big and in the middle! At the same time, the low-end offering was "For Small Groups" and the high-end offering was for "For Power Users," allowing people to self-select.

It's my belief that if all three tiers were given the same weight, a lot of people would have held off on making a decision, not sure if they were a small group or power user. It's that **uncertainty** that will send your site visitor heading for the hills.

To increase your conversion rate, limit the number of choices and promote one as your "most popular" or "best value" to reduce confusion and alleviate anxiety in your prospects.

Wrapping Up

Launching your website is actually the beginning, not the end, of the process.

Even with killer design, persuasive copy, and seemingly irresistible calls to action, not everything will be perfect. You might have limited your visitor's choices, selected photos to direct their gaze and attention, and used an action color perfectly, but there are still going to be places where your site fails. Where it leaks rather than converts.

And that's OK. In fact, it's to be expected.

By measuring and evaluating how people find your site and how people behave once they get there, you can continually improve its performance and conversion rate. You'll learn how to measure and analyze that traffic in the Evaluate section at the end of this book.

So go ahead and launch that baby! And in the next section we'll talk about how to bring the masses—or better yet, the qualified minority—to your website.

Attract

If you build it, they will come.

That paraphrasing of the famous line from *Field of Dreams* notwithstanding, just building a website isn't enough. You'll need to drive traffic to the site, and specifically *qualified* traffic. People who are ready to buy...if not now, at some point in the future.

There are plenty of ways to drive traffic to your website, including some "traditional" methods:

- Radio
- Television
- Print
- Billboards
- Networking
- Business cards

The list goes on. However, for the purpose of this book we're going to focus on the biggest **digital** opportunities for attracting the right type of visitor to your website.

You'll notice that I use the word "qualified" quite a bit in this book. That's because *anyone* can get traffic, and anyone can guarantee you traffic. For pennies on the dollar, some companies will literally hire people—often from distant countries—to visit your website, like your Facebook page, or watch your YouTube videos.

Don't believe me? Head on over to Fiverr.com and search for "website traffic." There are dozens if not hundreds of offers there. Will any of that traffic turn into customers?

Absolutely not.

As small business owners and marketers, we need to look past vanity metrics and pay attention to the numbers that matter: leads and sales. Sales come from quality leads, quality leads from quality traffic.

The three main traffic drivers we'll be discussing are:

- SEO
- Social Media, and
- Digital Ads.

Some businesses will find that one of these is far and away the most effective channel. Others may find that a blend of two or all three is the better approach. The important thing is to not get attached to the channel, but focus on the traffic, both in terms of the quality and the cost to bring that traffic to your site.

Many small businesses get hung up on social media. They want more likes on Facebook, more followers on Twitter, more friends on SnapChat. These are the vainest of all vanity metrics.

Yes, in general, a bigger audience generates more leads, but not always. And we seem to be entering a new phase in social media where the level of connection is more important than the number of people you're connected to.

Some businesses need as big an audience as possible, but that may not be true for your business.

A local hair salon in a small town is only going to need a small audience to survive and thrive. A business that sells monthly subscriptions to a piece of software, however, may need an audience of tens of thousands to turn a profit.

Be clear on what your business is capable of, and how many people you need to reach.

Search Engine Optimization (SEO)

So many small businesses get smitten with social media when they should really be focused on search. ***When people use search engines, they are actively looking for a solution.*** That's not the case when they see your post or ad on Facebook, because they turn to social media to connect with friends and family, or to get a laugh.

No one goes to Instagram or Twitter thinking, "I wonder how I'll save enough money for retirement?" or "where can I get an adult-sized Spider-Man costume by Thursday?"

When I review my clients' traffic reports, most sites are getting half to two-thirds of their traffic from search. Social, by comparison, is often an also-ran behind direct traffic, referral traffic, email, and campaigns. (We'll look at what that all means in the Evaluate section, I promise you.)

And most of that traffic is first-time visitors. In other words, if you want to get in front of new prospects, you have to have your SEO game down.

Depending on the type of search you do in Google (or, if you're from some alternate universe, Bing), you'll get possibly three types of results:

- Paid
- Local
- Organic

Displayed in that order.

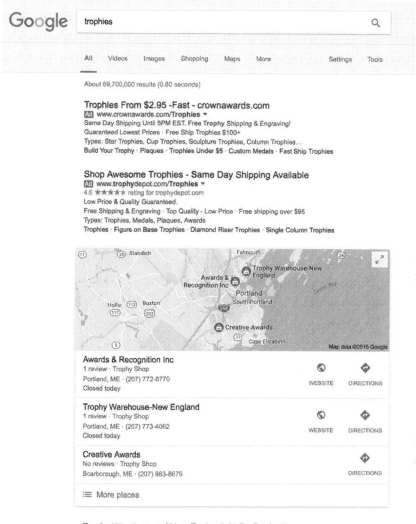

Google   trophies   🔍

All   Videos   Images   Shopping   Maps   More   Settings   Tools

About 69,700,000 results (0.80 seconds)

Trophies From $2.95 -Fast - crownawards.com
[Ad] www.crownawards.com/Trophies ▾
Same Day Shipping Until 5PM EST. Free Trophy Shipping & Engraving!
Guaranteed Lowest Prices · Free Ship Trophies $100+
Types: Star Trophies, Cup Trophies, Sculpture Trophies, Column Trophies...
Build Your Trophy · Plaques · Trophies Under $5 · Custom Medals · Fast Ship Trophies

Shop Awesome Trophies - Same Day Shipping Available
[Ad] www.trophydepot.com/Trophies ▾
4.6 ★★★★★ rating for trophydepot.com
Low Price & Quality Guaranteed.
Free Shipping & Engraving · Top Quality - Low Price · Free shipping over $95
Types: Trophies, Medals, Plaques, Awards
Trophies · Figure on Base Trophies · Diamond Riser Trophies · Single Column Trophies

Awards & Recognition Inc
1 review · Trophy Shop
Portland, ME · (207) 772-8770   WEBSITE   DIRECTIONS
Closed today

Trophy Warehouse-New England
1 review · Trophy Shop
Portland, ME · (207) 773-4062   WEBSITE   DIRECTIONS
Closed today

Creative Awards
No reviews · Trophy Shop
Scarborough, ME · (207) 883-8676   DIRECTIONS

☰ More places

Trophy Warehouse of New England, LLC - Portland
www.trophywarehousene.com/ ▾
Visit TWNE for laser engraving, plaques, trophies, acrylics, medals, bronze, trophy cases, plastic signs
and more! Our goal is to provide you with quality, on- time ...

Trophies - Crown Awards
https://www.crownawards.com/StoreFront/TRP.Trophies.cat ▾
Column Trophies. ... Trophies, Sport Trophies and Corporate Awards to suit all your trophy needs by
Crown Awards, America's largest manufacturer of Trophies. Crown offers SAME DAY SHIPPING (on
web orders placed by 5:00 PM EST) on in-stock trophies and FREE SHIPPING on all trophy orders ...
Column Trophies · Sculpture Trophies · 5 1/2" Vibrant Crystal Trophies

Trophies - Trophy Depot
https://www.trophydepot.com/Trophies/C4_1/ ▾
Trophies for All Sports and Awards Needs - Build Custom Trophies at Trophy Depot and Get Free
Shipping on All Trophies. Unbeatable Selection of Trophies ...

Let's take a close look at all three:

Organic results

These are what most people think of when they think of optimizing one's site for the search engines. This is the "meritocracy" of the page, where well optimized pages rise and poorly optimized pages, or spammy pages, sink.

Why certain pages rank higher than others is based on a wide variety of ever-changing variables...some of which we know, some of which we guess at, and some of which make us pull out our hair.

Local results

Certain searches pull up local results. For example, a search on "stretches" might pull up ten big blue links about different stretches people might do to get limber. A search on "yoga," on the other hand, might pull up three local studios in the "snack pack," some other local providers of yoga classes, and a Wikipedia definition of yoga.

Based on what Google believes is the searcher's intent, it will include local results.

If you have a local business, if you serve the local community, or you depend on tourist dollars, Local SEO is critical to your business.

Paid search

Google's brand name for this is Adwords. It's also referred to as PPC or pay-per-click. Which, when you say to someone, they hear "paper click," or even "paperclip," if they're especially hard of hearing.

It's also referred to as SEM, or Search Engine Marketing, which I find confusing since this is one place in search where it's advertising, *not* marketing.

Companies in the paid search arena are paying to appear on the first page of Google, bidding against other companies to grab your attention.

While some people may claim, "I *never* click on those ads," when you suggest they try Adwords, apparently not everyone feels that way. Google made $15.5 billion (with a b) in the first *quarter* of 2015.

There's a reason why advertisers of all sizes keep going back to Adwords: because it works and they can measure it.

We'll be looking at Paid Search more when we get to digital advertising.

How Search Engines Work

The primary purpose of a search engine is to provide relevant results to its customer, the searcher. It is *not* to send you reams of traffic. However, if you understand how search engines work, and how your ideal customer searches, you can certainly drive some of that traffic to your website.

The way search engines do this is by visiting, reading, and indexing every page, image, video, and document they can find on the web. They analyze these pages based on hundreds of variables. They then attempt to serve up these results in order of relevance based on the search terms.

These results may further be tweaked by the person's search history (a history buff may get different results than a Captain America movie buff when searching for "civil war"), device (mobile vs. desktop), geographical location, and a host of other features.

Some of the most important search engine ranking factors (according to Moz.com) include:

- Domain-level link features (quantity of inbound links, trust, domain-level PageRank)

- Page-level link features (PageRank, trust, links, anchor text distribution)
- Page-level keywords and content-based features (is the content relevant, does the keyword appear on page)
- Page-level keyword-agnostic features (content length, readability, uniqueness)
- Engagement & traffic (clickstream data, traffic, usage signals)

These are just a few of the elements that impact your rankings. For more details, I recommend checking out the data at moz. com/search-ranking-factors

There are countless books, videos, courses, and multi-day, multi-track conferences on SEO. I can't hope to compete with the breadth of knowledge that's out there, nor is that my intent. Instead, I want to arm you with the information you need to improve your website's search visibility or to be able to ask intelligent questions of an SEO agency.

Black Hat vs. White Hat SEO

People who are involved in SEO often talk about black hat vs. white hat tactics. Black hat SEO tends to look for holes in the search engines' algorithms to exploit. White hat SEO tends to follow the guidelines of the search engines, providing as much value to the site visitor as possible. And yes...there is plenty of room for gray in there.

Black hat tactics do work...for a while. And then Google sees what's going on and closes the loophole. Sometimes it means your site just loses that unjustified traffic, and other times Google penalizes sites and all your search traffic dries up!

If you're in this for the long haul, and I'm guessing that if you are reading this book, that describes you, then you want to put on your white hat. Companies that play around with black hat techniques eventually get burned, and then have to hire a white hat SEO company to get them back in Google's good graces. And that work doesn't come cheap!

SEO is Constantly Changing

To determine which web pages offer the most relevant results, search engines are constantly tinkering with their algorithm. The algorithm is the method that they use to determine how to provide searchers with the best results at the top of page one.

This is because as the search engines change to provide better results, webmasters adapt, making changes to their sites to rank higher. Search engines then reexamine the results, and make further changes, always trying to provide the most valuable, relevant results.

It's an ongoing battle that isn't going to end anytime soon.

Some of Google's bigger algorithmic changes have been named: Panda, Penguin, and Hummingbird. These updates changed the face of SEO, and many sites saw their traffic plummet because suddenly what had worked yesterday was now forbidden.

Because of this, writing a book about SEO is challenging. Any specific advice I write here might be outdated by the time you read this, or at least less effective. To that end, I've tried to put the most "evergreen" tactics in this book, and provide links and resources for those who want to dig deeper or get the latest information about search.

However, by following the guidelines, exercises, and recommendations in this section, you're very likely to see an improvement in your search engine visibility and search traffic to your website. Maybe not tomorrow, but certainly in the coming weeks and months.

Organic Search

When I talk to business owners about SEO, they often tell me that they want to rank higher in the search engines.

That response is too broad to be helpful. Instead, you should be focused on what *exact* questions ideal customers are asking at the search engines, and how can you appear higher for those specific searches.

Many searches are just too broad for the average small business to appear on the first page. It's going to be pretty difficult for you to rank for "books," or "travel," or "shoes."

However, you might have a better chance at getting found for "Boston antiquity bookstore," "Belize adventure travel," or "women's shoes in men's sizes."

Sure, you're not going to get the volume of search queries that the first group of words got, but assuming the words in the second bunch represent your offerings, you're much more likely to get higher rankings and qualified traffic to your site.

Over time, as you build up authority in your niche, you may see that you start to rank higher for some broader terms, but for now, focus on your niche. As they say in Internet marketing, "the riches are in the niches."

(If you live outside the US, just know that "riches" and "niches" rhyme in 'Murica.)

Breaking down SEO

To oversimplify SEO, the variables to ranking higher fall into two categories: on-page and off-page.

On-page optimization is all about the work you do on your website to use the very words (often referred to as keywords) your ideal customer is using at the search engines in specific, strategic places on your webpages.

Off-page optimization is all about getting quality websites to link to you, showing the search engines that you're providing content that's considered valuable.

Both types of optimization are important, and in the next few chapters you'll see step-by-step how you can optimize your site and climb up the rankings for your keywords.

On-Page Optimization

The goal of on-page optimization is all about matching the words on your webpage to the search your ideal customer is performing at the search engines.

We want to uncover those keyword phrases and place them strategically on our webpages, but not at the risk of readability or persuasiveness. In other words, we're still writing for people.

The process goes something like this:

- **Brainstorm:** this is where you want to generate as many keywords as possible that might lead prospects to your site
- **Test:** using software, you'll find out whether or not people are actually searching using these keywords, or if there are better choices out there
- **(Re)Write:** based on this new information, you'll create content that uses those words in strategic places throughout the site

Let's take a look at each one of these in turn.

Brainstorming Your Keywords

One of the first things I do when sitting down with a client for SEO is ask them two questions:

- What do you think are some of the phrases that your ideal customer would search for to find a product, service, or company like yours?
- What do you want to rank well for?

These questions might start a brainstorming session, but really they're not enough. Too many of us have spent too much time in our own industry. We're not thinking about the questions that a brand new customer—someone not familiar with our industry—might ask.

One of the exercises I recommend is to try and brainstorm keywords using five different perspectives. If you'd like to play along, open up your Lead Machine Workbook and find the section on Brainstorming Keywords.

Perspective 1: Products & Services

This is how we think of ourselves, and how we hope our clients think of us. It's the products or services we bring to market. It's the most obvious search term for most businesses, so we tend to focus on it.

Some examples might include:

- Maine web designer, Portland web design, WordPress web developer
- Dog trainer, puppy trainer, canine behavior classes

- Sales trainer, sales training techniques, corporate sales training
- Florist, flowers, wedding florist, Mother's Day gifts
- Bicycle tours, self-guided bike tours, bicycle trips in Tuscany

All businesses want to rank well for the results in this perspective, and with good reason. When people are searching for these terms, they're often looking for a result that will lead to a purchase.

Perspective 2: Problems

Now it's time to put yourself in your prospect's shoes.

What are the problems that you have helped your best customers solve or overcome? Many people search based on what they're suffering from. By reflecting their words back to them, you can capture some of that search traffic.

Some examples might include:

- Hair loss, receding hairline, Alopecia, bald spot
- Tantrum, screaming child, terrible twos
- Crabgrass, grub infestation, dead grass
- Bad back, back ache, lower back pain
- Sleeplessness, insomnia, waking up in the middle of the night

You may have many products or services, so try and come up with the problems that each solve.

Perspective 3: Benefits

This is just about flipping the previous perspective on its head. Some people search for problems, others for solutions. You want to generate a list of keywords that best describe the real or *perceived* benefits that people get after working with you.

Some examples might include:

- Healthy yard, green lawn, increased curbside value
- More leads, more customers, more clients
- Stress-free workplace, happy employees, lower turnover
- Well-behaved children, respectful kids, European boarding school
- Peace of mind, feeling of calm, sense of peace.

Again, some of these benefits may be tangible, some not. Some benefits may be perceived. If you can get to where your customer wants to be, you can meet them there.

Perspective 4: Features

If you've ever taken a sales course, you know that you never sell on features, you always sell on benefits. Well, on the web that's not always true. Often, your customers have done so much research they know more than you or your salespeople before the conversation even begins!

Some of these five perspectives will be more relevant than others, depending on your business, especially this one. If you can't come up with many (or any) relevant features, don't sweat it. Just do the best you can.

Some examples might include:

- 10 megapixels, 5 frames per second continuous shooting, ISO 100-12800 (expandable to 25600)
- Windproof, one-hand open, 15 color choices
- On-demand video content, lifetime access, private Facebook group for networking

- 100+ machines, spinning classes, 24/7 gym access
- Security cameras, round-the-clock doorman, safest neighborhood in Houston

The other thing to consider is that when someone is searching on features, it often means they've already done a lot of their research and they're looking to buy. They've got a mouse in one hand and a wallet in the other. Those are the kind of people we want to be in front of.

Perspective 5: Competition

Now, when I talk about competition, I don't mean that if you run a burger joint you should be brainstorming "McDonald's," or if you are a psychologist you should be writing down the names of the other doctors in your building.

Every business brings *something* to market. Imagine you own a gym. Why do people come? There are probably a few reasons: improve their health, become more attractive to the opposite sex, lose weight. Let's consider the lose weight option.

Is a gym membership the only way to lose weight? Of course not. They could get on a fad diet, or take diet pills, or buy a Thigh Master. In that case, those things are your competition. At some point, you may write a blog post like:

- Why the South Beach Diet Won't Get You into That Swimsuit by Summer
- Why Diet Pills Don't Keep the Weight Off (but a Gym Membership Will!), or
- How the Thigh Master Makes Your Butt Look Bigger

I'm using SEO judo...using my competition to attract attention to my own, better solution.

Get More Brains for Brainstorming

While you can certainly come up with this list of words by yourself, sometimes you're too removed, or too embedded in your own industry for this to be completely effective.

If you're part of a bigger team, bring in your sales reps. Ask them for the questions prospects are asking them during the sales process. Talk to your customer service reps, and ask them what questions or problems customer are having.

If you have customers, call up some of your favorites (and maybe one or two that you secretly can't stand) and ask them how they would describe what you do, the features and benefits of your products and services, and who or what they might turn to if you suddenly disappeared.

Very often you'll discover that people use your company for reasons you couldn't have imagined, or describe what you do differently than you would have thought.

Checking Out the Competition

Very often, some of your competitors will have already gone through a SEO project, so you might as well benefit from their investment!

Let's say you run a day spa, offering services like massage, reflexology, facials, and so on. You probably have a pretty good idea of who your competition is. Visit their sites and make note of some important elements of their home pages:

What is the title tag of the page? This appears outside the page in the tab on your browser. If you can't read the whole thing you can hover over it with your mouse and often the full name will appear. Pay close attention to the first few words in the title.

Are there any headers? These are usually bigger and bolder than the regular copy. Are there any good keywords here? Ignore headers like "Welcome to Enrique's Day Spa" but pay attention if it reads, "Phoenix Day Spa and Massage."

What do the first few sentences look like? Are they keyword-rich, too? What words are they using here?

What pages are they linking to in the body copy? If they're linking to the page on reflexology and the links don't say "Read More" or "Click Here," or something similarly helpful but generic, those words were probably chosen for a reason.

What do the meta-tags contain? This gets a *little* tricky, but I know you can do it! Meta-tags don't appear on the website, but they do appear in the source code. Every browser has a way of displaying the source code. Often you can right-click and one of the options will be View Source. Sometimes you'll see the option in the View menu (Chrome) or the Develop menu (Safari).

Once you're looking at the code, don't panic! Just do a find (CTRL-F on a Windows machine, Command-F on a Mac), for "meta." Often there will be two results, "meta-description" and "meta-keywords."

Meta-description is what search engines use for the black descriptive text below the big blue links. Although these have little to no search value (depending on who you ask), they can persuade a searcher to click on your result, so they're important. Pay attention to any keywords that may be included.

Meta-keywords are very important to SEO...if this was 1997. Now they're completely ignored. However, some people still use them. Pointless for them, good for you. They basically are a list of the keywords that they want to rank well for, giving you more ideas.

After checking out your known competition, you may want to Google some good descriptors for your business: day spa, massage, Swedish massage, deep tissue massage, reflexology, etc. Find the top few results for each of these search terms and run through the same exercise.

If you have no nearby competition, do the identical search in a bigger market. In fact, checking out similar businesses in a very competitive market—L.A., NYC, Chicago, etc.—can give you even more insights, as these companies may have had to hire very expensive SEO firms to put them at the top of Google for their given area.

What Is Your Competition Bidding On?

If your competition is spending precious budget by bidding on keywords in Google Adwords, chances are they feel strongly about those particular keywords. If only there was some way to discover what those keywords were!

Here comes SpyFu [theleadmachinebook.com/spyfu] to the rescue. SpyFu is a paid service that can provide you reams of information on your competition and how they're spending their Google Adwords dollars. (And, of course, reveal your ad spend to your competition!)

If you put your own URL into SpyFu, it will return who it believes to be your nearest competition based on overlapping keyword usage. Alternatively, you can put in your competitors' domains to see what they are targeting and how much they're willing to spend to get in front of that audience.

Market research indeed!

Organizing Your Keywords

By now you should have a healthy list of keywords to use. The next step is to organize them by the type of services you offer.

For example, you might offer home inspections for new home buyers, environmental audits for current homeowners, and mold removal for commercial buildings. You'll need to take your list of keywords and organize them into those categories, whether they represent Products & Services, Problems, Solutions, Features, or Competition.

Once that's done you can start to test which of these keywords—or even ones you haven't considered yet—are going to be the seeds from which you grow your most effective copy.

Testing Your Keywords

The first time I heard about the "curse of knowledge" was in Dan and Cliff Heath's book, *Made to Stick*. The idea is that as experts in our field, it's sometimes difficult to explain ideas, teach, or even to understand the problems of people who don't have our knowledge.

In brainstorming keywords, this can lead to assuming your ideal customer knows all that you do and uses the jargon of your industry. Imagine the plastic surgeon who writes great content about rhinoplasty while his ideal customer searches for information on nose jobs. Or a marketing company talking about KPI while a prospect searches for "what should I be measuring?" Or a sandwich maker promoting gyros when the locals search for subs.

While Google and the other search engines are getting better at understanding intent through semantic search, it's always best to use the exact language your ideal customer is using. Even if Google directs them to your site, if your language doesn't match up with theirs, they will feel a disconnect and the trust will be lost.

The *Entrepreneur on Fire,* John Lee Dumas, once told me that assessments with short-answer questions are powerful tools on websites, because the people filling them out give us the exact language we can use to market to other people.

Why haven't you achieved your fitness goals?

- I can't seem to find the time.
- I'm too busy driving the kids to afterschool activities.
- It's too easy for me to quit when I don't have a workout buddy.

These phrases can be spun into copy on home pages, squeeze pages, blog posts, and social media updates.

Similarly, you can "interview" the people who have searched for your solutions through a few free and paid search terms. You can uncover the language they used to see which of your brainstormed terms are likely to be most effective, and to discover new phrases that your curse of knowledge prevented you from knowing.

While there are dozens if not hundreds of similar tools out there, I'm going to focus on the ones we use that are perfect for small businesses.

Google's Keyword Planner

This is the go-to tool for finding how popular a given search term is (whether a lot of people are searching for it) and how much competition you can expect (whether a lot of sites are optimizing for it.)

It's important to understand that this tool is provided by Google for free to help advertisers bid appropriately on Google Adwords, the sponsored links that appear at the top of many of Google's search results pages (we'll get more into that in the PPC section later).

In other words, the competition rating is about the advertising, not the organic search. However, if advertisers have been bidding up a keyword phrase, it's likely that the competition for the organic results is also fierce.

Keyword Planner is free, but you will need to set up a Google Adwords account. You don't have to pay for anything unless and until you are ready to start bidding on some keyword phrases.

To get started, grab your organized keyword list and head on over to [theleadmachinebook.com/keywordplanner].

There are a lot of ways to use Keyword Planner, and Google is constantly adding new features, while removing some others they feel are no longer effective. For the purposes of this book, I'm going to take you down the path I use most often, but feel free to explore the other tools Google offers.

Once you've logged in, choose *Search for new keywords using a phrase, website or category*. (If you don't see this exact choice, find something similar. Google often tweaks its tools.)

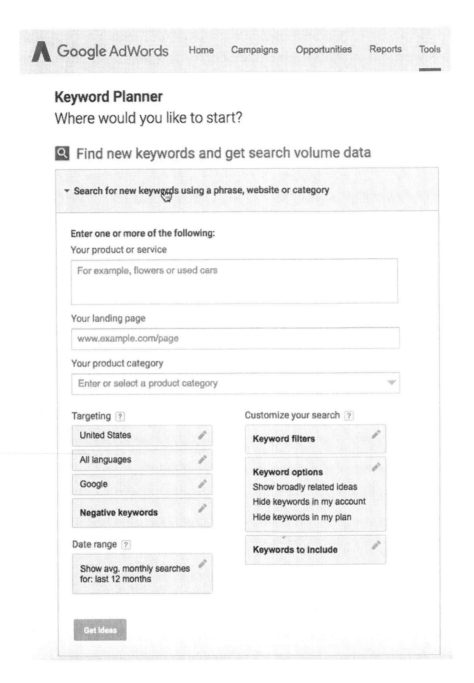

You'll see a section for adding your products or services. This is where you want to enter one of the groups of keywords you came up with.

You might enter "dentist, periodontist, teeth whitening, dental implants, gum disease," for example. I could have also entered a landing page and/or a product or category, but I kept these blank for now.

I also looked at the targeting options and noticed that in the negative keywords, Google had pre-populated this field with "jobs." This means it will ignore any searches that were job related. Unless I'm trying to build up my job opportunities page for my dental practice, this is good. We'll get more into negative keywords in the PPC section.

You can further customize your search and your results, but for right now let's "let it ride" and just click *Get Ideas*. We can always come back and play around with our search if we're unsatisfied with the results.

Google has been good enough to organize the results into Ad Groups: collections of related phrases. Some of the Ad Groups included:

- Whitening (5, 166,800, medium)
- Gingivitis (12, 105,360, medium)
- Dentistry (17, 50,240, medium)
- Veneer (9, 85,030, high)
- Periodontal Disease (17, 37,300, medium)
- Whitening Best (19, 30,590, high)
- Implants Cost (19, 41,340, high)

The information in the parentheses represent the number of words in the Ad Group, the average number of searches, and the competition for bidding on these phrases, respectively.

Some things you'll notice: although we didn't include "gingivitis" or "veneer," or even any part of those words, Google realized that these are related searches to the words we included. This means we should be creating content around these phrases, assuming those are services we offer.

Also, "Whitening Best" and "Implants Cost" are both highly competitive ad buys, probably because these are profit centers for dentists...either because they're uncovered and patients pay out of pocket, or they reimburse at higher levels.

Lastly, "Whitening Best" has a fraction of the search volume of "Whitening," but is more competitive. Why would that be? My assumption is that advertisers have realized, by reviewing their ROI, that people searching for the *best* teeth whitening solutions are more likely to make a buying decision at the website.

Important note: I've realized over the years that "best" is one of those magic words on the Internet when it comes to search. Years ago, when I wrote my first article on content management systems, I did a quick keyword analysis to determine what I should title my article. "Best CMS" and "Best CMS for small business" were two of the top results. I retitled my article "What's the Best CMS for Small Business?" and for years those two phrases were two of the most popular keywords driving traffic to our site.

Reversing that, when I wanted to buy a Bluetooth speaker for my iPhone, I Googled "best Bluetooth speaker." I did the same with "best sound canceling headphones."

I believe this gets at our desire to get answers quickly when searching. How can you leverage the "best" search that your ideal customer is doing? A list of "best restaurants in San Bernardino" for your bistro? A compilation of the "best short stories of 2016" for your bookstore? Or a rundown of the "best ways to save money for retirement" for your accounting firm?

Digging into an Ad Group

While we should probably check out all relevant Ad Groups, let's start with "Dentistry."

The list is sorted by relevance, but we can also sort by Avg. Monthly Searches, to give us a sense of what the most popular search terms are. I see:

- Family Dentistry (14,800, high)
- Dentistry (12,100, medium)
- Sedation Dentistry (8,100, high)
- Kids Dentistry (3,600, medium)
- Gentle Dentistry (2,900, medium)
- Laser Dentistry (1,900, medium)
- Sleep Dentistry (1,300, high)
- Aesthetic Dentistry (1,300, medium)

Looks like a lot of people would prefer to sleep through their appointment!

When I look at this, I'm probably going to ignore "dentistry." It's a very broad term that would be difficult to rank for on its own, but we'll still be targeting it by using it with some of the other modifiers like "sedation," "kids," "gentle," and so on.

And even though "Family Dentistry" looks to be harder to rank for compared to "Kids dentistry," I'm probably going to lean towards promoting family over kids based on the search volume. My page title may end up looking something like:

Houston Family Dentistry: A Dentist for Kids and Parents Alike!

I added the location modifier because I believe that most people are going to be looking for a local dentist. In fact, on another search I did, "dentist near me" had 135,000 monthly searches.

"Near me" is becoming a very popular modifier, but I wouldn't recommend optimizing a page for this term. Google most likely understands it as a request to find a dentist near the searcher, not for a page optimized for the term "near me."

What this exercise does is help you determine what are likely to be the most effective search terms for your website and your business. Continue to do this for all of your grouped search terms, using this information to determine which phrases are going to be most effective.

We're going to use these phrases to develop something called our Keyword Matrix, and also as the cornerstone of our content marketing.

Google Trends

Another favorite tool of mine is Google Trends [theleadmachinebook.com/trends].

Trends provides historic data on searches, and allows you to compare and contrast multiple keywords to see which should perform best.

One of the most dramatic experiences I had with Trends is when I was doing some research into the hair restoration industry. The people I was talking to used the phrases "hair restoration" and "hair replacement" interchangeably. I was curious to see which one would be more effective as we developed a content marketing strategy.

As you can see here, restoration beat out replacement by a hair. (I can hear your collective groans as I write this.)

However, I was a little concerned that both seemed to be trending downward. Google Trends doesn't share exact numbers with you, but it does give you a sense of overall direction. Because of this, I decided to throw in two additional terms, "hair loss" and "alopecia," which is a condition that causes early hair loss, especially in women.

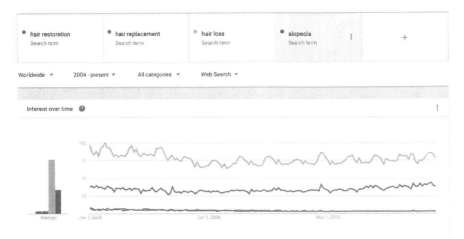

Now that's a pretty dramatic change. "Hair loss" was by far the most popular search term. And "alopecia," although in a distant second, was still significantly more popular than the previous two keywords.

So, what's the takeaway here?

Well, if I want to reach the widest possible audience, I want to focus my attention on hair loss. That's where the majority of people's focus is, and if I want to get in front of these ideal customers, I need to be creating content that's all about hair loss, not restoration or replacement.

If I scroll further down the page, there's a section that will give me additional content ideas based on the most popular searches and the top rising searches.

Related queries ❓		Top ▼ ⋮
1 loss of hair	100	▓▓▓▓▓▓▓▓▓
2 hair treatment	65	▓▓▓▓▓▓
3 hair loss treatment	65	▓▓▓▓▓
4 hair loss women	65	▓▓▓▓▓
5 weight loss	45	▓▓▓▓

Top searches and top rising searches are another great area to generate keywords for your site.

Top rising searches are also often great opportunities for blog posts. These are the emerging trends that you should jump on before your competitors do. It's been my experience that if I write on a topic that later becomes popular, my blog post will often rank well for a long time. This is in part due to the fact it was published earlier and in part due to the fact that other people link to my blog post as a resource.

So, even if my company doesn't offer a shampoo to battle hair loss, I can still create valuable content around it that will help me get in front of my ideal customers. I might write an article on "Do Hair Loss Shampoos Really Work?", "What's the Best Hair Loss Shampoo?" or "Read This Before Using Any Hair Loss Shampoo."

Once they get to my page, I can show them that I have a better solution, or at least an alternative solution, to their problems.

In this case, I know that "hair loss" and "alopecia" are great keywords for my Problem perspective. I can also add "hair loss shampoo" as a Competition keyword, assuming that's not in my product line.

Pro Tip: Don't ignore "hair restoration" or "hair replacement" just because they don't get the search volume! People are still searching on them, so you could certainly use these phrases in your content, even if the main focus is "hair loss."

Also, people who are searching for restoration or replacement are probably further along the research trail, and closer to making a buying decision. I'd use "hair loss" to attract a wider audience and get them signed up for my free email newsletter, but I'd use "hair restoration" to target people closer to a buying decision.

Creating a Keyword Matrix

We use the phrase "keyword matrix" at flyte to describe the framework that will help you optimize a page for the search engines. There are strategic places on a webpage where you should concentrate your efforts on optimization.

Here are the four fields of the matrix:

Keywords

When we're putting together a keyword matrix for a client, we list all the keywords, monthly searches, and competition we're targeting for a page. I prefer to keep my pages as focused as possible, only targeting 1-2 keywords, but our list usually includes up to 10 keywords. This is to help with modifiers (location, other descriptors) and alternatives (less popular, but still searched on, phrases).

Page Title

Search engine experts often disagree on just about everything, but they all agree that the page title is the most important element on the page for ranking well.

The title doesn't appear on the page itself. Instead, it appears on the browser tab outside the page. It's also what populates the big blue links on the search engine's results page.

Search engines also tend to give more weight to the first few words in the title, so make sure you frontload your title with your best keywords. Some experts like to put their company name up front, but I put it at the end of the title, or not at all, on most pages. This is because I figure if someone is searching for my company name, they're going to find me. However, if someone has no idea who I am, but they're looking for "Maine web design" or "Portland Maine SEO firm," I want to come up first.

I do make exceptions for the About page or the Contact page, where I'll often lead with the company name.

In the early days of SEO, people would "keyword cram" their titles. That means that they would stuff as many of their keywords as they could in the title tag with the hope that this would boost them to the top of the search engines. For example:

Bill's Bakery: Bread, Crusty Bread, White Bread, Whole Wheat Bread, Muffins, Donuts, Baguettes, Bagels, & Scones

Sadly, it worked!

Now, search engines are more sophisticated, and they're looking for more focused, readable titles. Bill would be better served with a title like:

Bangor Bakery: Home-baked breads, muffins & bagels | Bill's Bakery

Bill could then build individual pages about all the wonderful baked goods he sells, each with its own keyword rich, narrowly focused title.

Often I'll use the colon or pipe character to try and work in more potential keywords:

Chopstick Instructions: How to Use Chopsticks

I feel this allows me to cast a wider net when I'm trying to get in front of people who search differently, but are looking for the same thing. Consider this when pulling keywords from both the Problems and Solutions perspectives.

Another consideration is the length of the title. Google tends to display the first 50-60 characters of a title, so you may want to make sure you paint inside the lines. Otherwise your titles will get cut off with a series of ellipses...

Some CMS platforms will add your company or website name as a suffix to the end of each page title, which unwittingly pushes you past the 60-character mark. This can usually be disabled in the settings.

Meta-Description

While people may debate how much direct impact—if any at all—your meta-description has on your ranking, it can influence whether searchers click on your result or not. And Google does pay attention to which links gets clicked. If more people click on your link in a search result, your prospects improve. If few people click on your link, your rankings might fall.

Your meta-description can include calls to action, a slogan, or a reason why searchers will find what they need by clicking on your link.

You don't need to include your keywords in your meta-description, but chances are some or all can be worked in. Most search engines will show 150-160 characters of your description, so make sure you don't go any longer.

Pro Tip: If you want to get the phone ringing, you can include your phone number in the meta-description. If people are searching on their phone and see your result, the phone number in the meta-description is hotlinked, meaning they can call you even before they visit your site!

Headers

Headers (and subheaders) tend to be bigger and bolder than the copy that surrounds them. Most pages start with a header (often an H1 tag) and then use subheaders (often H2 or H3 tags) to break up the rest of the text and make it easier for scanning.

You definitely want to work your best keywords into your headers and subheaders. I often try to compliment, but not replicate, my page title.

When we're developing the keyword matrix we'll often include the header, although the subheader is usually dependent on the body copy.

The Content Intake Packet (CIP)

Speaking of which, there are things we don't include in the Keyword Matrix, but they are critically important to the success of the page. One of the documents we provide to clients is called the Content Intake Packet, or CIP.

I often describe it as a "dolled-up Word doc" where we've pre-populated the titles, headers, and meta-descriptions, as well as included the most important keywords the page should be built around.

Here are some of the fields that are included in the CIP, that you need to consider as you're creating your own search engine optimized copy.

Body Copy

Copy is simply the words on the page. I try and get my best keywords in the first one to two sentences, and definitely in the first paragraph.

I work them in a few more times, but only if it sounds natural. Sometimes I come up with a partial usage, as there are only so many times you can say "Telluride real estate" before it sounds ridiculous.

I work them into my subheaders, too.

Links

Make sure that you're creating good, relevant links from one page to another. But don't use links like Read More or Click Here. Instead, put your keywords in the links.

This helps search engines see how your website is organized. Also, since links are often bold or underlined, your visitor's eyes will be drawn to them, pulling them deeper into your site.

Alt-tags

If you've ever rolled over an image and seen a yellow box with a description pop up, you've seen an alt-tag.

Although alt-tags have been abused by site owners in the past, loading them with highly-searched but completely irrelevant words, alt-tags are one of the ways that search engines make sense of an image. I wouldn't bet my SEO on alt-tags, however, they can increase your chances of getting found, especially in an image search.

Developing an Optimized Page

You'll want to pull out your sitemap now and start assigning keywords to specific pages. Let's imagine you run a vacation rental property service in Arizona. Groups that come to Arizona to golf are your best customers. Therefore, you'll probably have a page detailing your Golf & Stay packages.

In doing your keyword research, you've uncovered a few relevant results that show promise:

- Golf packages (1,300 monthly searches)
- Vacation rentals (135,000 monthly searches)
- Golf vacation packages (1,300 monthly searches)
- Arizona golf resort (2,900 monthly searches)
- Luxury condos (880 monthly searches)
- Luxury vacation rentals (2,400 monthly searches)

Even though "vacation rentals" has the most searches by far, it's also a broader, more competitive term. We should definitely use it, but it's not descriptive enough to feature on this page.

Also, I'm surely going to talk about "luxury condos" and "luxury vacation rentals," but again, I don't feel that this is the driving force for this page. Here's my first attempt:

Title: Arizona Golf Vacation Packages | AZ Luxury Condos

Reasoning: Start my title with my best keywords. After the pipe character I'm going to put in another search term. I also know that some people will abbreviate Arizona. I don't think that luxury condos will help so much with search, but it may pull in some extra clicks.

I could have used my company name here, but unless it's a well-known brand, it probably won't help.

Meta-Description: Looking for a golf & stay vacation package in sunny Arizona? Spend your day at a top-ranked golf resort and your night in our luxury condos. Call 800-000-0000

Reasoning: Building on my title, this is the descriptor text below. I want to paint a picture using some keywords as appropriate. I included a call to action (call), and included a phone number so searchers could just click to call.

Header: The Best Arizona Golf & Stay Vacation Packages

Reasoning: I'm restating my title without exactly copying it, and I'm using "Best," one of the magic words on the Internet. :)

The Rest of the Page

Once I've got these four items—keywords, title, meta-description, and header—in place, I'll begin to write my copy.

The purpose of webpage copy is to persuade the visitor to take a desired action. The purpose of SEO is to attract the visitor in the first place. Good copy can do both.

I will work some of my best keywords into the first couple of sentences, and repeat them a few times throughout the page. I'll use some of my secondary keywords, and broader keywords, in subheaders, such as **Stay in Our Luxury Vacation Rentals**, and **Choose from Arizona's Best Golf Resorts.**

I'm also going to create keyword-rich links to other pages, such as mentioning our exhaustive list of Arizona golf course reviews and linking those words to that page. I'm also going to find other pages on my site and make sure that I link back to this page as appropriate.

Finally, I'm going to make note of what images I want on this page, and make sure I have appropriate, keyword-rich alt-tags for each one.

Keeping Your Sanity with SEO Copywriting

One thing to keep in mind is that keyword research is often as much art as it is science. Also, nothing you create is chiseled in stone. If I create the page and it doesn't rank as well at the search engines or pull in as much traffic as I would like, I can continue to tweak the title, header, and body copy to improve the results.

I can create more keyword-rich links from other pages to this one. I can work to get more inbound links from other websites.

In short, I can continue to improve my rankings once the page gets out there.

Spotlight on Yoast

There are a number of plugins and tools that help you with your onsite and onpage SEO. My personal favorite is Yoast SEO for WordPress. [theleadmachinebook.com/yoast]

It's available on a freemium model, meaning you can download and install it for free, and unlock more features and support through the paid tier. Even the free version is incredibly powerful, however, and a great way to get started.

The Yoast plugin does many tasks, including connecting to social media, creating default titles and meta-descriptions, and creating sitemaps. However, I want to focus on the optimization tools it gives you for each page and post.

When you're writing your copy for a web page (or blog post), the Yoast plugin offers some powerful features.

The Yoast plugin appears below the window for writing your blog copy. The first section is the Snippet Editor. This shows you a preview of what people will see at the search engines. Using the editor, you can improve both the title and the meta-description for this page, making sure it's the right length, it's keyword-rich, and it's sending the right message.

Yoast SEO

Help center ▾

★ Go Premium

● Readability   ● Keyword: *google analytics fil...*   +

👁 Snippet preview

How to Set up Google Analytics Filters for Better Traffic Reports
www.takeflyte.com/google-analytics-filters/
Google Analytics filters improve your traffic reports by removing unnecessary data. This post shows how to block your company traffic for better reports.

🖊 Edit snippet

🔑 Focus keyword

google analytics filters

☰ Analysis

- The SEO title contains the focus keyword, but it does not appear at the beginning; try and move it to the beginning.
- This page has 0 nofollowed link(s) and 2 normal outbound link(s).
- The focus keyword appears in the first paragraph of the copy.
- The keyword density is 0.8%, which is great; the focus keyword was found 4 times.
- The meta description contains the focus keyword.
- In the specified meta description, consider: How does it compare to the competition? Could it be made more appealing?

Below that, you can enter your focus keyword. (The paid version allows you to enter multiple keywords here, a nice upgrade.) Once you've entered that keyword, Yoast will provide you with feedback and suggestions for improvement.

For example, you might be warned that:

- The focus keyword doesn't appear in the first paragraph of the copy. Make sure the topic is clear immediately.
- A meta description has been specified, but it does not contain the focus keyword.
- You have not used your focus keyword in any subheading (such as an H2) in your copy.

But it's not all bad news. Yoast might also congratulate you on a job well done:

- The page title is between the 35-character minimum and the recommended 65-character maximum.
- The focus keyword appears in the URL for this page.
- You've never used this focus keyword before, very good.

Being an automated tool, not all the helpful suggestions will be...helpful. Still, it's a good way to see if you're making any obvious mistakes that can be quickly remedied.

Off-Page Optimization

Imagine you've got a business trip to Portland, Maine. (Lucky you!) You're looking for the best lobster roll, and you survey ten friends. Seven of them recommend Lobster Shack A, and three of them recommend Lobster Shack B.

All things being equal, you'll probably go to Lobster Shack A.

However, what if the first group had vacationed in Maine, but never spent any real time there? And what if the second group, the minority, was made up of a native Mainer, a well-respected host of a Food Network show, and a woman who wrote a book called, *In Search of the Perfect Lobster Roll?* Now, you might be more likely to go to Lobster Shack B.

This is an approximation of how inbound links work for search engines. Search engines take a look at the number and quality of inbound links a site gets as part of their algorithm. Getting an inbound link is like getting someone to vouch for you; it's a vote of confidence.

However, once some site owners realized that Google and other search engines were rewarding them for inbound links, they went out and used a whole range of tactics to get more inbound links. Some of these tactics were legit, such as creating valuable content and getting listed in appropriate directories.

However, some were more questionable, such as exchanging links for the sake of exchanging them or paying for inbound links.

The long-term strategy that should keep you out of hot water is to create insanely valuable content that people want to link to and share.

The Varying Value of Inbound Links

Now, not all inbound links are created equal. Just like in the example above, the people who grew up in Maine, were well-known foodies, and had an expertise in lobster rolls, had more street cred than those who didn't.

So, what makes one link more valuable than another? Well, there are many factors, but here are a few of the most important ones:

Popularity. How popular is the linking site? Does it have a lot of inbound links? Search engines give more weight to links coming from popular sites compared to less popular ones.

Context. Is the site related to yours in terms of context? If you repair bikes, it's more valuable to get a link from a bike club rather than a taco stand, all other things being equal.

Anchor text. These are the words in the links. It's better if someone links to you with your best keywords or brand name as opposed to "click here."

Trust. This is how much trust the site has built up based on the quality of inbound links and other factors. This is different than popularity, because a government site or a university site may not have a lot of popularity, but it does have trust.

Now, you may have little to no control over these factors, but if you're going to actively try and get links from other sites, this might help focus your activities.

Counting Your Inbound Links

New sites will obviously have few to no inbound links. Even established sites may not have many inbound links if link building wasn't a priority of the site owner.

The first thing you should do when you start off-page optimization is to see how many inbound links you have. I use Moz's Open Site Explorer (OSE) for this. https://moz.com/researchtools/ose/

Open Site Explorer is a free tool, but if you're a Moz subscriber, additional features will be unlocked.

When you enter in your URL, OSE will provide you with a lot of data, including:

- **Domain Authority:** An estimate on a scale of 1-100 on how much authority your domain has at the search engines
- **Page Authority:** An estimate on a scale of 1-100 on how much authority your page has at the search engines (if you didn't specify a page, it defaults to your home page)
- **Established Links:** How many domains are linking to you, and how many times all these sites are linking to you (a site may have multiple pages linking to you)

OSE will also show you who is linking to you, the anchor text (the words that link to your page) they are using, a "spam score" of the linking page, as well as page and domain authority for the linking page. The number of linking pages that OSE shows you is limited in the free version.

How Many Inbound Links Do I Need?

I'm not aware of any magic number of inbound links, and I'm sure it depends on industry and competition. If pressed for an answer, I'd want to have a minimum of fifty unique domains pointing to my site. That doesn't mean I'd stop at fifty, just that it might become less of a priority at that point.

To get a better sense of how many your business needs, you could run the same OSE report on your competition, *including* those businesses beating you on some of your most coveted keywords, to determine how many inbound links they have, thus setting the bar for you.

How Do I Get More Inbound Leads?

There are certainly a number of ways to quickly get inbound links, but they generally won't help your business. Remember: you are not in the business of getting inbound links. You don't get paid for the number of inbound links to your website. Inbound links are **only** important as a tool to improve your search engine visibility and to create more paths to your website.

If you're looking for legitimate, value-based ways of getting more inbound links to your site, here are some good places to start:

Member-based organizations. If you belong to any member-based organization, like a Chamber of Commerce or an industry group, it's likely they have a place on their website where they link to members. Make sure you're listed there.

Directories and guides. Very often, vertical directories rank well for local search. For example, if you search for "Baltimore psychologist," you may well get a directory or two of Charm City psychologists in the top spots. It might be worth your time to get listed in a few of the more popular directories for your targeted keywords. Some may offer free listings, but to get your domain linked from the directory, you may need to pay an annual fee.

People linking to your competitors. Chances are, if people are linking to your competition, they may be open to linking to your site as well. This requires a little bit of legwork. You'll want to see who's linking to your competitors using a tool like OSE, and then track down the site owner for each of these sites, and email them a request.

Chances are they won't add you the first time you ask, and some will never add you. It helps to write a nice, personal note, explaining that their site visitors might enjoy a particular blog post or resource on your website.

Link building companies. I've never enjoyed actively going out and getting links for my business. It's time consuming and I feel there are better ways to invest my resources. That's where link building companies come in. They'll do all the hard work on your behalf.

Please be aware! There are probably more disreputable—or at least inept—link building companies out there than good ones. Do your homework. See what other people are saying about them. Check references. Ask *how* they generate inbound links and what type of sites you can expect to get links from.

Guest blogging. This is probably my personal favorite, and the one I use the most myself. Many blogs and websites are actively looking for content to fill their editorial calendar. You're looking for inbound links and to get in front of an established audience. The answer is guest blogging.

You generally won't get paid for guest blogging, but you will get at least one link from the article to a page on your website.

The more trust the site has built up, the more valuable that link. The bigger and more relevant the audience is, the more people you can get in front of.

Another variation of guest blogging is being interviewed on a podcast. Almost all podcasts have show notes, which is basically a blog recap of the show. It's customary to have a link to the interviewee's website or other material.

This is a nice alternative if you don't like to write or you're pressed for time. A good blog post will often take 4-6 hours to write, where a podcast interview will often take only 30 minutes of your time.

Should I Link to Other Websites?

There is some evidence that when you link to external resources, you "leak" some of the trust you've built up at the search engines. Meaning the more you link out, the worse your ranking will be.

There's also some evidence that linking to trusted resources helps put you in a "good neighborhood," increasing your search engine rankings.

But no matter what I tell you, Google could easily change its algorithm by the time you read this, making my advice harmful. So here's what I recommend: link to external resources when it's warranted.

If there's an external resource that will provide extra help for your site visitor, you should link to it. If there's an external resource that will buoy your argument, you should link to it.

If there's an external link that you're linking to because you think it will help your search engine ranking and that's the *only* reason you're linking to it, don't.

One bit of external linking that I generally recommend against is linking to a member organization. A number of my clients over the years have wanted to establish their credibility or authority with the logo of a member organization or a certifying agency.

First off, most lay people have no idea who these organizations are, so they don't really add a whole lot of credibility. But if you're adamant that you need these logos on your home page, then don't link to the websites behind them!

Most of these sites offer directories of their members—basically a quick listing of all your competitors! After all the hard work of getting a visitor to your website, why would you want to shepherd her away...and to a complete listing of all the people who do what you do?

If you *must* link to the organization's website, don't do it from your home page. Bury it deep on a Resources or Links page where no one will ever visit it. ;)

Lastly, when linking to other websites, you might want to have that site open in a new window or tab, so they're not *truly* leaving your site.

Other SEO Factors

Creating valuable, keyword-rich content and getting other relevant sites to link to you will make a huge difference in your search engine visibility and the amount of search traffic you can drive to your website.

However, there are other factors at work. Some you can control, others you can't. Here's a quick rundown of a few of them.

Site speed. This is growing in importance. Slow load times don't just frustrate your users; they lower your overall rankings. Google even provides site speed reports and recommendations in Google Analytics.

Mobile friendly. This currently has more impact on people who are doing a mobile search than all searchers, but since a growing number of people are probably using a mobile device to search, this is important.

SERP clickthrough rates. Are people clicking on your site when they see it in the results? A higher clickthrough rate can lead to higher rankings.

Length and readability. Search engines want to return results that are at an appropriate reading level and long enough to provide value. A recent study showed that the average length of first page Google results was 1,890 words!

Social shares. Quantity and quality of tweets, Facebook shares, etc.

Real-world citations. Existence and quality of verified, real-world info on your company.

Age of domain. Domains that have been in use for a while rank higher than newer domains.

Please note that these are not listed in any particular order of importance, and they are believed to be true "all other things being equal." For example, a newer domain will outrank an older domain if the content is better quality, a closer match to the search, and has more inbound links.

Another important thing to keep in mind is that search ranking factors continue to evolve. What's true today may not be true tomorrow...or at least may be less true. There's already evidence that because of semantic search, exact match keywords in the title may be less relevant than they have been in the past.

Social Media

Social media has proven an incredible disruptor over the past few years. It has evened the playing field between small business and big corporations by giving us a place where we can establish our credibility, connect with our audience, and build our business.

It was especially beneficial early on, when fast-moving, nimble entrepreneurs were jumping in and experimenting, while big corporations waited on the sidelines, running everything through a team of lawyers.

Times have changed. Social media isn't the game changer it used to be. First off, everyone has a Facebook business page, from your dentist to the convenience store down the street, from global soft drink companies to the local firehouse. Competition for eyeballs and engagement is fierce.

Second, the platforms have matured, and made it more difficult for us to reach our audiences. Just a few years ago, a business on Facebook could expect that 70%-80% of their fans would see a post. Now that's down to a paltry 1%-5% for most pages. In other words, if you have 1,000 fans (likes) for your page and you post something, you'll be lucky if 50 people see it as they're scrolling through their feed.

The advice from these platforms: you should be advertising with us.

Third, the novelty of seeing your favorite pizza place or hotel chain on social media has worn off. It's not news that you have a social media presence, it's the expectation. When people *can't* find you on social media is when there's a problem.

How to Get Started with Social Media

For businesses that have no presence in social media, getting started can be intimidating.

- What platforms should we be on?
- How much time is this going to take?
- Who's going to take ownership of this?
- How much is this all going to cost?
- What if someone says something mean about us?
- What if something goes wrong?

Let me try and make this easier.

When it comes to which platforms you should be on, you should start small. Focus on the platform or platforms where your audience already spends time. Don't try and be a mile wide and an inch deep. Better to get really good at one platform before expanding.

If you're going to manage this in house, it's best to have one person lead the team, even if it's a team of one. Don't just hand it over to an intern or entry level employee because "they're young and they get it." Just because someone uses SnapChat doesn't mean they know how to use it for business. They may understand the difference between a "snap" and a "story," but not understand your business goals or audience.

You can also work with an outside agency to manage some or all of your social media. Of course, there's a cost to outsourcing this work. There's also a cost in having your employees run your social media.

Chances are, if you're doing something worthwhile, *someone's* going to take offense. We'll talk in more detail about how to manage the trolls as well as the legitimate customer complaints that take place in social media.

How to Keep Up with Social Media

One of the biggest questions I get from small business owners and entrepreneurs about social media is how to keep up with it all. If you run a small business, you know: you're already wearing too many hats as it is...how are you going to manage your brand across Facebook, Twitter, LinkedIn, Pinterest, Instagram, a blog, a podcast, YouTube, and who knows what else?

While we'll be taking a look at a lot of these social media sites and platforms in the next several chapters, no book can provide up-to-the-moment social media marketing advice. Facebook has changed so dramatically so many times that any advice I give may be outdated a week later.

Although Twitter and LinkedIn don't roll out changes quite as frequently, it's still difficult to keep up. And then there's always some new channel popping up that everyone seems to be talking about.

For most small businesses, *you don't need to be everywhere.* In fact, it could be detrimental to your brand to overextend yourself. If you're on a platform, there's a certain expectation that you are paying attention to that platform. If someone tweets to you about a problem they're having with your wait staff, or software, or telephone system, and you're not there to respond, you look like you don't care.

Start small. Start with one, maybe two platforms. Start where you know your audience is already hanging out. Once you've mastered those platforms, then consider expanding outward.

Just remember that social media is not a silver bullet. It takes time and probably money to make an impact in social these days, and the landscape is constantly changing. That's why I think it's important to ask yourself these questions before jumping into any social platform:

- How do I reach my ideal customer here?
- How do I engage my ideal customer here?
- How do I convert my ideal customer here?

How do I reach my ideal customer here?

If your ideal customer isn't on a given social media site, there's no business reason why you should be there either. Personally, you may love LinkedIn, but if you're trying to reach stay-at-home parents, this may not be your playground.

Even if they are on the platform, you need to ask yourself if this is a good place to engage with them. Seemingly *everyone* is on Facebook, but if you're trying to reach hospital comptrollers, they may not want to hear from you when they're trying to catch up with family and friends as they unwind from a busy day.

On the other hand, if you have a platform you're not in love with, but your audience hangs out there, you need to be there. Maybe to engage with them, maybe to field their questions, maybe to let them vent about a bad customer service experience.

How do I engage my ideal customer here?

Each site has its own "rules of engagement."

On platforms you own, such as a blog or podcast, it's up to you to create content that will attract and engage your audience.

On social networks, it may be a balance between sharing tips, advice, and inspirational quotes, and listening to what your audience is saying and responding to it.

You might be able to engage through public posts, or you may get better engagement through private messages.

As a business (or entrepreneur), you need to be respectful of people's personal space. I've seen too many entrepreneurs jump into social media with an over-inflated sense of entitlement. People who believe that just because they *can* do something, they *should* do something.

This includes sending Facebook invites to people around the world for a local event they're throwing. Or tagging everyone they know in a post to build awareness for something they're doing. Or "private messaging" fifty people at a time to tell them about a new eBook they've got for sale.

Social media exists because people are social. Don't break the social contract by being "that guy," or you'll soon find yourself ostracized or even exiled.

How do I convert my ideal customer here?

I don't recommend you try and "sell" someone in social media. I understand it can be done, but I feel that social media's true strength is in building trust, credibility, and your brand.

You wouldn't go to a real world networking event with a blank contract in hand, trying to get everyone and anyone to sign it would you? (Please say no, please say no...) So, don't act that way online, either.

If you do go to networking events, you probably spend time getting to know people, understanding what they do, and what their pain points are. If there is something you can help them with, you might mention that after you learn about them, and then you might suggest that you meet for coffee or at your office so you can talk in more detail.

That's how I recommend you approach "conversion" when it comes to social media. Get to know people—their hopes, their aspirations, their hurdles—and when there's an opportunity to help them, bring them back to your website (your online office) and *then* you can talk business.

Social Media: Platforms vs. Networks

When business owners ask me where they should start in social media, I often recommend that they pick two sites: the best platform and the best network for their business.

Let me explain what I mean by that:

Social Media Platforms

Back in the early 90's when I was studying in London, I would often go out to Speaker's Corner on Sunday mornings. Anyone could stand up on a soapbox—or the equivalent—and spout their personal, professional, or political beliefs.

Crowds of varying sizes would gather, and occasionally respond to the speaker...anything from an "Amen!" to "You're an idiot," or worse.

To me, that's the best IRL example of a social media platform.

It's a place where you can speak your piece, build an audience, and get engagement and feedback. Some online examples include:

- Blog
- Podcast
- Online video (YouTube being the best example)
- SlideShare (think YouTube for PowerPoint presentations)
- Webinars (yes, these can be social!)

Some benefits of social media platforms include:

They increase your visibility. All of the platforms above will help you get seen by more people. They all have SEO benefits, either inherent or easily added. They all have social media benefits, allowing people to easily share your content. They all have content that can be reused, repurposed, and recycled, meaning you'll get more out of your marketing.

They let you tell your story. This can come in handy in a number of situations. Telling your story can help personalize your company or brand. Telling your customers' stories can help inspire others and attract people to hire you to help them achieve similar successes. And, if you ever get into a PR mess, they can help you tell your *side* of the story.

They allow engagement. On your blog, YouTube or Slide-Share, people can leave comments that lead to conversations. On your podcast, you can have show notes (which is really just a blog post) where people can also post comments, or you can have people ask questions which you answer on your show. On webinars you can constantly ask your audience for questions, have surveys, and engage with people...even if they can only hear your voice.

They have greater reach in B2B. Although this is becoming less of an issue, many corporations block access to social media sites at work. Even for those who don't, many people you want to reach in businesses aren't checking Facebook or Twitter during the workday. However, many of them are Googling stuff for their jobs.

If they're Googling stuff, your blog post, video, or podcast could be one of the top results for that search! Creating valuable content on a social media platform may be your way of being introduced to your ideal customer.

Social Media Networks

This is what most people think of when they think "social media." Facebook. Twitter. LinkedIn. Pinterest. Instagram. SnapChat.

These networks are places where people go to relax, share, catch up with friends, vent, kvetch, and occasionally do business.

One important thing to keep in mind is that **you don't own any of these networks.** (Mark Zuckerberg, if you're reading this, please ignore.) You can expand a lot of energy building a following on any of these platforms, but you don't control the access to your audience.

Facebook could change their algorithm (again) and suddenly you disappear from the newsfeed. Twitter could go out of business and suddenly you lose access to your 5,000 followers. LinkedIn could become the next MySpace, and suddenly everything you've built up there becomes completely irrelevant.

However, the same is true in real-world networking. Unless you're throwing the party, you're not in control. You can connect and engage, but if you don't get a business card (or their digits), you may never see them again.

This is why I strongly recommend engaging people through social media networking, but bringing them to your website and/or getting them on your email list.

Still, there are many benefits for social media networks:

They offer great engagement. Because there's already an audience, and conversations are already going on, it's a great place to meet your ideal customers and engage with them.

They let you listen in. Social networks offer many ways to listen and many different things to listen for. You can listen when someone comments on your page or post on Facebook. You can listen when someone uses your handle or brand name on Twitter. You can listen for your competitions' brand names. You can listen to see what else your ideal customers' talk about when they're not talking about you (which is most of the time).

They allow self-promotion. Go easy on this one, but you can certainly promote a new product, launch, or event. Just try and keep it native, meaning that it should feel like the type of conversations that are happening already in the network.

They drive traffic. I use social media for both personal and professional reasons, as do most entrepreneurs and small business marketers. When I'm using social media for business reasons, *one* of my end goals is to drive traffic to my website or squeeze page.

This is so I can capture someone's contact information, get them on my email list, or lead them down a funnel.

I do this by creating valuable content *outside* of the network and then promote it through links and images within the network.

What's Next

Next we're going to take a look at some important social media platforms and networks that can help you reach your ideal customers and generate more traffic and leads for your business.

Let's go!

Blogging

Of all the digital marketing tactics I've used over the years, I find blogging to be the most effective. Probably because it's so versatile.

It's great for driving traffic to your website because it makes it so easy to create optimized copy for the search engines. It's great for social media because it allows you to start or facilitate a conversation, as well as giving you fodder to share on social networks.

It's great for establishing your credibility. So many of my clients over the years have come to us because they did a Google search which led them to our blog. After reading and seeing our expertise, they contacted us.

It's invaluable for getting journalists to contact you when they're looking for an expert in your industry. I wrote one blog post on podcasting...*one!* And *Inc.* magazine reached out to me and said they understood I was a podcasting expert and they wanted to interview me for the magazine.

I told them I was, but I couldn't speak right then and scheduled our interview for two days later. Then I ran out to the bookstore, bought two books on podcasting, and read them cover to cover.

Two days later I had the interview, nailed it, and got mentioned in *Inc.*!

Lesson is: don't necessarily believe expert advice in *Inc.* ;)

Another time I had written a series of blog posts on QR codes, when those were a thing. CNN.com reached out to me to talk about how marketers could use QR codes and ended up featuring me in an eight-page article that included links back to our website.

Blogging is also great for email marketing. You can use the content in your blog to give people an incentive to stay up to date by signing up for your email list. The content in your blog can be promoted to your email list, driving more repeat traffic to your site.

And your blog can house other types of content: your podcasts, YouTube videos, slide decks, and almost anything else you want to share with your audience.

Your blog also helps keep your website neat and orderly. New content doesn't have to mess up your carefully thought out navigation. Instead, you just continue to add it to your blog, putting it in the appropriate category or tagging it as necessary.

What You'll Need to Succeed with Blogging

Convinced yet that blogging is good for your business? Great! Let's get started. There are three things you'll need:

The right blogging platform. There are plenty of blogging platforms out there, but in my opinion, nothing is as good as WordPress. It was originally built as a blogging platform, and it's only become more robust, evolving into a full-on CMS. That means that you can host your blog easily within your website, which is how I'd recommend you set it up.

To be master of your own domain. With apologies to *Seinfeld*, it's critical that you own the domain you host your blog on. Although I see this less today than in years past, I still run across blogs with URLs like mycompany.blogger.com or mycompany.wordpress.com.

In these cases, you're building authority for blogger.com or wordpress.com, respectively, **not** for your own domain or business. If this is how your blog is set up, you need to either move your blog to your website or buy an additional domain and point it to your blog.

This is critically important for SEO.

To be committed. Not to an asylum, mind you. But you need to be committed to the process. If you're just starting a blog, it's important to work towards building a critical mass of posts. I generally recommend weekly posts for six months before changing up your editorial calendar.

Blogging success rarely comes from just a handful of posts. Instead, it comes from regularly creating valuable content that helps your ideal customer overcome their problems or satisfy their needs and wants.

Getting Started

Although blogs are pretty fluid and unstructured, there are some ways to help organize the content.

Categories. These tend to be the major themes of your blog. While some businesses have dozens or dozens and dozens of categories, I recommend trying to keep them to a more manageable number.

The categories should reflect your major offerings or areas of expertise, and should align on some level with the primary navigation items on your website.

Blog posts can be added to one or more categories. The default category for WordPress is Uncategorized. The first thing you should do when setting up your blog is delete or rename this category. If you want a catch-all category, give it a more unique name: The Kitchen Sink, Odds & Ends, Widows & Orphans, or

Square Pegs. I'm sure you can come up with something clever that reflects your business.

Tags. These are added to individual posts. Often they relate to something specific in the blog post that's not an overarching theme of the blog. If you had a superhero blog, Sidekicks might be a category, but Robin, Bucky, or Bob, Agent of Hydra, may only warrant a tag.

(I'm sorry; I let my nerd show.)

Blogging for SEO

Every time you create a blog post, you create a web page. Every time you create a web page, you're creating another opportunity to be found at the search engines by your ideal customer.

But it's not just about writing a blog post. You need to be creating blog posts that answer the questions your prospects are asking at Google, using *their* language. You need to be treating blog posts like you did web pages in the previous SEO section.

That means doing your keyword research. It means working your keywords into titles, meta-descriptions, headers, body copy, links, and alt-tags.

But the reason I love blogging so much for SEO is how flexible it is. I don't need to worry how a new piece of content is going to impact my website or navigation, I just create it. I assign it to the appropriate categories, tag it, and publish it.

On our own website, we have the newest blog posts teased from the home page automatically, making it easier for the search engines to find the fresh content on our site and index it.

Blogs aren't just good self-optimizers; they can be used to optimize any of your web pages. This is especially helpful for e-commerce sites, which often struggle in search.

The Electromagnet Theory of Blogging

People ask me all the time how they can improve their search engine visibility, and often my answer is "blogging." To explain how this can work, let's go back to 7th grade science.

You were handed a battery, a copper wire, and an iron bar (often a nail). You connected either end of the copper wire to the battery and wrapped it once around the iron nail. What did you get?

That's right! An electromagnet! (Did you know, or did you just re-read the title of this section?)

A very ineffective electromagnet. But the more times you wrapped that copper wire around the nail, the more powerful, the more attractive, the magnet became.

You can use that same model to attract people to your website.

Let's say that there's a keyword you'd like to rank well for. Let's say it's "restaurant kitchen equipment." If so, you'll want to write a series of blog posts about restaurant kitchen equipment. About the best-reviewed kitchen equipment for restaurants. About the most cost-effective pieces of restaurant kitchen equipment. About which pieces of equipment are the most dangerous. About how to find deals on used equipment. About how to get equipment serviced. About the OSHA rules around the equipment. About the best cleaning supplies for the equipment. And so on and so on.

And on each of these posts, you're going to create keyword rich links to your web page on restaurant kitchen equipment. You're not always going to use the same exact phrase. You're also going to create links to related blog posts.

Each of these links acts like one more lap around the iron nail. Each one helps your content become more attractive to the searchers and the search engines, establishing your credibility in this vertical.

Where to Get Ideas
for Your Blog

If you've been blogging for any length of time, you've suffered from "Blogger's Block." In fact, one of the reasons a lot of entrepreneurs don't start blogs is because they're afraid they won't know what to write about or they'll run out of topics quickly.

There are plenty of places to turn for inspiration, and what follows is just a select few resources that I use when I can't think of what to write about.

Google Trends

In Google Trends, pay special attention to the Rising searches at the bottom of the page. This section is pure gold for bloggers. It lets you know about emerging trends in your industry...what people are beginning to search for.

The reason the journalists reached out to me as an expert was because I was an early adopter when it came to blogging about those topics. Because I was early, other bloggers linked to me to bolster their own arguments that these were important topics, worthy of blogging about. That helped me rank higher in the search engines and put me in front of those journalists.

What I accomplished by accident, you can accomplish purposefully!

Quora

Another great resource for blogging is Quora.com. While there are many Q&A sites on the web, Quora tends to be a great resource for blog-worthy questions.

Do a quick search on your topic or interest, and you'll find questions that will generate new ideas for blog posts. Just run them through Google Keyword Planner to make sure you're using the language your customers are searching for.

BuzzSumo

BuzzSumo.com is a great resource for finding proven content winners. Search on your keywords and find some of the most shared, most viral content on the web. This will give you an idea of what type of content will work for you.

I'm not suggesting you steal from these sites! That's bad for SEO *and* your eternal soul!

13 Blog Post Types

The battle isn't over once you know what to write about...sometimes it's how you present the information to make it interesting and intriguing to your audience.

How-tos and Tutorials

The how-to is the most powerful of all the blogging archetypes.

Think about it. Why do we go to the web? Sure, it could be because we want to find out the latest sports scores, catch up with old friends or visit IMDb to find out who that familiar actor was on last night's *Law & Order SVU*.

But often it's to learn how to accomplish something—change our oil, get debt under control, connect Search Console to Google Analytics, etc.

Your prospects and customers are the same. They have a problem, and you can help them solve it by creating a step-by-step post that walks them through a solution.

A lot of bloggers and business owners are afraid of the how-to post. They think, "If I show them how to do my job, why would they hire me?"

If a 500-word post or a 2-minute video can expose your entire business expertise, you might be in the wrong business.

How-tos and tutorials establish your credibility and expertise. Even if a reader chooses to do it on her own, at least she knows about your business now. She may consider you for other opportunities down the road.

Lists

List posts streamline information into a numbered list that's easy for your readers to read, share and put into action. They speak to our desire to find the best information in the shortest amount of time.

Some bloggers hate list posts because they feel they've been done to death, but there's no denying they're effective.

All you need to do is visit any newsstand and check out the cover stories of popular magazines: 10 Exercises for Tighter Abs, 101 Ways to Save for College or The 5 Best Family SUVs.

Resource or Link Lists

Very similar to the list post is the resource post. The difference is that resource posts curate other people's content (albeit usually in a list format).

Resource and list posts are perfect if you're just learning about a category. You're probably gathering resources for yourself, so why not share them with your readers?

Don't have the time to research? Resource posts are an easy type of post you can hand off to your intern or virtual assistant to do the research for you!

Alternatively, you could ask experts in your field for a tip, then curate those answers into a new blog post. One of the most popular and shared posts I ever put together was "69 List Building Tips from the Experts."

Many times when you share a list of tips from experts, they'll promote your post to their audience for you.

Cheat Sheets and Checklists

Often what your audience seeks from you is direction. If they have a question, they want someone to answer it—or at least get them on the right track.

While not too different from a how-to, these posts tend to focus on how to do something more efficiently and ensure nothing is forgotten.

As a bonus for your readers, you could add a printable PDF. It's up to you whether you want to brand that PDF with your company information or put it behind an email registration.

Reviews

There are two kinds of review posts: A straight review of a product or a compare-and-contrast of multiple related products.

Many blogs have made a business out of straight reviews of products and services. You can find review posts of books, software, local restaurants, and everything in between.

I should tell you, though, that reviewing products regularly may get you free, unsolicited samples from people looking to get coverage in your blog, so be prepared for free gifts! (If you ever needed a reason to review bacon on your blog, I just gave it to you.)

As consumers, we rarely if ever have the time to fully test every product in a category ourselves, so we do research on the web. Offer a head-to-head comparison of products to drive a lot of traffic to your site.

Controversial Posts

If you want interaction, take a controversial stance on a subject your audience is passionate about.

I used to run a blog under the brand The Marketing Agents...a precursor to my Agents of Change blog. One of the first posts I ever wrote there was the case *against* responsive web design, the popular approach to mobile-friendly design. To this day, it's one of the most shared and commented-on posts I've ever written.

But I have to warn you, if you do write a controversial post, be prepared for some angry comments from the other side. If you don't have thick skin or an excellent therapist, this post type may not be for you.

Infographics

I can't count the number of times an infographic has bailed me out of writer's block. They're easy to find and interesting to read.

You can find an infographic by searching on a certain topic, like "dog infographic" or "restaurant infographic."

When you find one you like or you think will appeal to your readers, there's usually some code that you use to easily embed it into your post. Then it's just a matter of adding a paragraph or two to provide context for your readers.

People love sharing infographics and easy-to-digest statistics, so it's a good bet they'll share your post with their audience.

Podcast Show Notes

The business case for podcasts has been made many times before, and rightfully so. They're a great way to build a passionate audience for your product or service.

As a bonus, behind every great podcast are the show notes, which you can publish as a blog post. You can use a full transcript of the show or just highlight the main themes.

Publishing podcast show notes not only gives additional information to your listeners, it introduces your podcast to your readers. It's also the type of post you can easily outsource to a transcription service, virtual assistant or co-worker.

Videos

If you're creating videos and posting them to YouTube, that's great! You're taking advantage of the second-largest search engine, gaining access to over a billion people who watch YouTube videos every month and building rapport with the people who watch your videos.

But why stop there? You can reap even bigger rewards by embedding your videos in an article on your own blog.

Surround your video with related contextual copy, or just include a transcript of the video to create a valuable blog post. Either way, you'll be getting more views for your video and increasing the time visitors spend on your blog.

Interviews

Interviews are a great way take the pressure off of you to create content. Talk to industry leaders, satisfied customers, or a random guy at the coffee shop to get a fresh perspective you can share with your audience.

When you put your post together, you can provide the interview as text, audio, or video, depending on which option best fits your (and your audience's) needs.

And hey, your interviewee may choose to share the post with his or her audience once it goes live.

Guest Posts

Getting outside experts to contribute to your blog gives you fresh content without having to write it all yourself. Sites like Social Media Examiner, Convince & Convert and Copyblogger have successfully used guest blogging to build massive audiences.

However, you can't put your guest blogging program on autopilot. You'll still need to set up editorial guidelines, vet the quality of the work and make sure each post is original.

As you accept guest posts, keep in mind that often the guest blogger's goal is to drive traffic from your site to theirs. But by regularly providing amazing, valuable content, your readers will keep coming back to your site for more.

Blog Series

Sometimes an idea is just too big for a single post.

One way to maximize the impact of a "big idea" is to break it into parts. A series helps build anticipation for the next post and improves your SEO if you link from one post to the next in a natural, organic way.

"Dear Abby"

This is probably my favorite type of post. If you've been in business for any length of time, people are asking you questions. Via email. Over the phone. In person.

And these are just the people who are savvy enough to ask *you*. Imagine all the people who don't know who to ask, so they ask Google! You can be Google's go to resource for that question.

I'll often take a good question, generalize it, and then turn it into a question and answer blog post. What makes these posts especially powerful is that you can phrase the question just like the question that your ideal customer is asking in Google.

Crafting an Effective Blog Post

Once you've identified your topic and keywords, and have an idea of what style of blog post you want to write, it's time to get to work.

Some bloggers prefer to write directly into a blogging platform like WordPress, while others write offline in a Word doc or Evernote. I've tried it both ways, but generally I prefer to write in Evernote and then copy and paste my article over to Word-Press. Once it's in WordPress I add a header image and any other images, videos, or slide decks as appropriate.

Also, the formatting might need a little tweaking, and I generally add my links in at this point.

While there are many ways to create a blog post, I'll walk you through my method. I can't say that I do all these steps every time, but I try and do as many as feels right.

Title

I start with my title, even if I end up changing it. This comes directly from my keyword research and I generally place my keywords as close to the beginning of the title as possible. For example, with my keywords in bold:

- **Saving for Retirement**: Getting Employer Contributions
- How to **Train Your Dog Off Leash**: Tips and Tricks for Puppy Owners
- What's the **Best CMS for Small Business**: WordPress vs. Drupal

Let's pause for a moment and geek out on some blogging nuances. Above, I'm talking about the page title. The page title appears outside the web page in the title tab. It's also the big blue link in the search engine results page.

The post title, by comparison, appears within the blog post. It's actually a header...usually an H1 tag. It's also what gets shared when someone clicks on one of those ubiquitous social sharing buttons.

By default, WordPress, and most blogging platforms, makes the page title the same as the post title. However, I prefer to create different titles for the page and the post. To accomplish this, I have installed Yoast's SEO plugin. (Most SEO plugins can do the same.) I create a page title that's focused on SEO and keywords, and then a post title that's more clever, and focused on getting more shares and clicks.

Header

I try and reword my title in a way that's likely to get shared. For the three examples above I might create the following headers:

- How to Get Your Employer to Feed Your Retirement Fund
- 5 Steps to a Well-Behaved, Off Leash Puppy
- The WordPress vs. Drupal Smackdown (You'll Never Guess Who Wins!)

Opening Paragraph

I try and work my keywords into my opening paragraph, often in the first couple of sentences. If it doesn't flow naturally, I just create an intro paragraph whose purpose is to introduce the main theme of the post. If you *still* can't work in your keywords, you're probably not writing the right post.

Some bloggers like to start with questions, which is a great approach. I might ask 1-3 questions that get to the pain points of my reader's situation:

- Do you feel like you're not saving enough for retirement? Do you wish there was a way you could contribute more, but you can't afford to put aside any more money right now?
- Does your puppy go crazy the second you let him off the leash? Are you tired of the disapproving looks of parents as they pull their children closer to them at the park?
- Are you looking to take control of your website, but you don't know what's the right platform for you? Do you wish you someone would take the guesswork out of choosing the best CMS for your small business?

Another approach, which can be used in conjunction with the question approach, is to explain exactly what the post is going to be about and what people can expect to learn by reading it.

Some bloggers recommend including a link to another post or external article in the first paragraph. My feeling is yes, but only if it's warranted.

Subheaders

Subheads, often H2 or H3 tags, are great ways of breaking up the article and making it more "snackable." They're also a good place to put in some more appropriate keywords. If you're creating a list or resource post, subheads are a great way of introducing the next item.

Body

The rest of the body should be easy to read, regardless of the length. That means breaking up the text as much as possible. To accomplish this, I recommend:

- Short paragraphs
- Bulleted lists (like this one!)
- Bold and italicize important ideas (this also has a small SEO boost, so consider emphasizing your keywords, but don't kill yourself over it)
- Links (where they make sense)
- Images (besides the header image, use other photos, charts, and illustrations, as appropriate, to demonstrate different ideas
- Audio, video, and slide decks from SlideShare

I'm not recommending using *all* these elements in every post, but using a few of them can make your post easier to read. Big blocks of text will turn off most site visitors.

Links

Linking to other pages, either on your own website or externally, shows that you're part of the web. Search engines often look at outbound links favorably, especially if they add value to the reader.

I try to link to at least one other blog post or web page on my own site, as well as any appropriate offsite resources that make sense.

Calls to Action

You're not blogging for your health! Your blog is here to help you grow your business. To that end, you should be blogging primarily on topics where you can help your readers out or add value to their lives.

What do you want them to do when they finish reading your post? Visit a product page in your online store? Fill out a contact form? Pick up the phone?

Don't assume they know what to do next. They may have come from a search engine and they don't realize you have a white paper on how to get matching funds from your employer, or you have a paid video series on off-leash dog training, or that you build CMS-powered websites for small businesses.

Your calls to action could be in-post links to appropriate pages on your site, big buttons, signup boxes, or whatever else will help guide the site visitor to take a step that will help them in their business or their life.

Images

These days, *all* blog posts should include a photo or other image at the top of the post. A high-quality image adds visual appeal and makes your post look more professional. It also makes it more likely that your post will be shared across social media platforms like Pinterest and Facebook. When it is shared, the image is shared with it.

For a while it was popular to have an image take up half the column at the top of your post. This makes the column with the copy thinner, which makes it easier to read. (This is why newspapers have thin columns...anything over 12 words across causes reader comprehension to go down.)

By the time your reader got to the wider column under the image, they were hooked.

These days, column-spanning header images are popular, often with text overlays. This is so you can send a message with your photo, giving people even more reason to read the post.

With modern CMS platforms, you can even specify which image should be shared on which platform. This comes in handy since the preferred image size and ratio differs from platform to platform.

For our Agents of Change website, we create at least two versions of each image: one horizontal one for Facebook and Twitter, and a more vertical one for Pinterest.

Odds & Ends

Before I hit publish, I take care of a few more items:

Slug: The slug is the part of the URL that follows the domain name. In the domain www.takeflyte.com/marketing-advice, "marketing-advice" is the slug. It's a great place to put your keywords and should be kept as short as possible.

Categories & Tags: I add the post to the appropriate categories and put in any tags that make sense.

SEO Check: Using an SEO plugin, I double-check that I've optimized my post and look at any issues the plugin has raised. Some are valid, some can be ignored. This is also where I can change my page title and create a meta-description.

Excerpt: On some websites, the "Excerpt" field is used to create a description for the post that will show up on the home page or other places. If you're not sure if your site uses this, you can ask your webmaster.

Preview: Although WordPress and other blogging platforms let you create your blog in a WYSIWYG (what you see is what you get) manner, there are always differences between the admin version and the published page. The preview will let you see how your site visitors will see your post.

Publish!

Now that everything has been checked, go ahead and hit publish to make your post live!

Congrats! Break out the bubbly! Your work is done, right?

Not quite. All successful bloggers know that you need to do some promotion around every single post.

Here's a checklist to get you going:

Sharing buttons. Have you ever tended bar? What's the first thing a bartender does when he starts his shift? He puts money in the tip jar! People are much more likely to tip a bartender when they see that other people have put money in the jar (even if it's just the bartender).

The same is true with your social sharing buttons. Go ahead and share your post across all the platforms you have buttons for. Besides alerting your followers on these platforms, it also acts as "social proof" if the share buttons have a counter attached to them.

When I get to a blog that has goose eggs (zeroes) across the top of every blog post, I think to myself, "Not even the *author* can get behind these posts!"

The flip side of that is when I see a blog post with hundreds of shares. Then I feel that if so many other people shared it, there must be some value to it.

Scheduling social media posts. I'm not a big fan of automation in social media, but I do believe that it's beneficial for small businesses and entrepreneurs to use scheduling tools to share content...both their own and other people's.

Using a tool like Hootsuite, Sprout Social, or Buffer, you can schedule your tweets, LinkedIn updates, and other social media posts. However, I'd recommend *against* using these tools on Facebook. Facebook tends to "de-emphasize" your posts from 3rd party tools like these, so it can make it harder to reach your audience this way. Instead, you can just go to Facebook and schedule posts using the Facebook scheduler instead.

Email your list. This is probably the most important element to drive traffic to your site. Your opt-in audience *wants* to know when you publish new content.

There are some email platforms out there that will publish your blog post automatically to your email list. However, I prefer to send out a more personal email, teasing the content in the blog and asking if people want to go check it out.

It takes a few more minutes, but it drives more traffic to my website where people can comment on my blog post or share it through the social media sharing buttons.

Create links from other posts. One way that you can add legitimacy to your new post is by linking to it from a related, popular post on your blog (or other blogs, if you contribute to and manage other blogs). Here's a ninja tip on how to do just that:

Visit Google and type "site:www.yourdomain.com keyword" where "www.yourdomain.com" is your business website and "keyword" is the keyword your new post is about.

For example, if I've just written a new blog post about webinars on my blog, I might search for "site:www.takeflyte.com webinars." This will return all the webpages on my site about webinars. I'll find a result near the top, go to it, and find a natural way to link from the old, established post to my new post. I'll make the link keyword-rich and I'll try and get it as close to the top of the page as possible.

Common Blogging Questions

I love blogs, and I love presenting on blogging. There are certain questions I almost always get during Q&A. Here are a few of my favorites:

How often do I need to post?

I used to feel that businesses should be blogging about three times a week. That made a lot of audience members queasy.

I've come over to the school of quality over quantity. It's better to have one amazing post a month than thirty posts that are filler.

Instead of cranking out content, you should invest more time in researching your post, polishing your post, and promoting your post.

How long should a blog post be?

It was popular for a while to say blog posts should be 300-500 words max. However, there's a lot of research now stating that pages and posts that are over 1,000 words long get the most page views, comments, and shares. They also make up the bulk of Google's first page of search results.

What if I get negative comments on my blog?

Years ago I presented on blogging to an innkeepers' association. One of the innkeepers asked me: "Rich, I have 5,000 people stay at my inn each year. No matter what I do, not all of them are going home happy. Why would I let people disparage me on my blog? I have enough headaches with TripAdvisor and Yelp."

My response was, that was *exactly* why you should allow negative comments on your blog. At least at your blog, you have home field advantage. If someone wants to complain about your business, there's no shortage of places to go. With your blog you know they're commenting and you can respond.

In the case of an innkeeper who might have a disgruntled guest, I would probably apologize for the experience, offer to make it up to them (a free night stay, etc.), and provide your personal contact information.

It's unlikely the guest will come back to the blog, but everyone who visits after that post and sees your response will see how seriously you take customer satisfaction.

(You should also practice this behavior on TripAdvisor, Yelp, and other relevant review sites.)

What if no one comments on my blog?

It's nice to get comments. It proves that someone is actually reading your blog.

However, comments aren't customers. You can't pay the bills with comments. At least, that's what the electric company told me. If you're looking to build community, the volume of comments is an important metric, but if you're just looking to improve your SEO and generate leads and your blog is accomplishing those tasks, then don't worry about it!

Podcasting

The benefits of blogging are obvious. Thanks to your optimized posts, you can rank well at the search engines and drive high quality traffic to your website.

Blogs have a huge potential user base...basically anyone who knows how to use the internet and Google stuff.

There's easy adoption: people already know how to read and Google, so once they get to your blog post, they can consume your content with no additional special skills or knowledge.

And assuming your blog is part of your website, your blog readers are right where you want them! That makes it easy to shepherd them over to your contact form, rate calculator, or e-commerce store.

The Case Against Podcasting

Podcasts, on the other hand, don't appear in the search engine results, unless you're taking the extra step of transcribing your shows or putting together optimized recaps and posting them as show notes (read: a blog post).

Pew Research has shown that the current user base for podcasts is quite small, even among adult internet users.

It's more difficult for people to listen to podcasts for the first time. If you want to listen at someone's website, you have to hope you're not going to be disturbing a co-worker or family member by listening. If you want to listen on a mobile device, you have to have special software to listen and subscribe. Many people who have the software as part of their iOS don't even realize it's installed, or know how to download, listen, or subscribe to a podcast.

When someone is listening on a mobile device there's no guarantee they're at your site. Unless you add show notes there's no place to leave comments or simple way to provide feedback. There are no links to click, and even if there were, you might drive off the side of the road looking for them!

So why would you invest your time in podcasting?

The audience is growing.

I love having a podcast. Yes, there are fewer potential listeners (currently), but I've found the ones that do listen are quite passionate. There's also the potential that podcasts will grow in popularity as companies make it easier to onboard new listeners.

The Podcast app is now standard (and un-removable) on iPhones. Android phones are *finally* getting a native podcasting app of their own. Many new cars are coming with podcast platform Stitcher Radio built in, just like satellite radio was built into new cars previously, leading to an influx of new satellite listeners. Also, other audio-focused companies like Spotify and Audible have started offering access to podcasts as well.

You can literally get inside someone's head.

The human voice is a powerful tool. Speaking to someone through a car stereo or earbuds gives you access in a way no other channel does. I've had people tell me it feels like they know me after listening to a few episodes.

Podcasts can reach people where other channels can't.

Many, if not most people, listen to podcasts when they're driving, at the gym, or mowing the lawn. Three places where they can't be reading a blog or watching a video (safely), but it's easy to do these tasks while listening to a podcast.

Also, many people are "auditory learners." They prefer audio books over written books because that's just the way they prefer to learn.

It's inexpensive to turn your podcast into a blog post.

There are services that will transcribe your entire episode or just put together show notes which can be put into a special blog post with the audio from the show.

People *subscribe* to your podcast.

Through services like iTunes or Stitcher, people can subscribe to your podcast. That means that once you post a new episode, it automatically downloads to their phone or computer. (Usually. There are different settings depending on your device.)

It has the benefits of any social platform.

It allows you to establish your expertise. It allows you to attract and build an audience. It allows you to easily create content.

It helps you generate income.

When most people think of monetizing their podcast, they think of getting sponsors. That's not a bad approach, but sponsors generally pay depending on how many downloads you get (that's the most watched metric in podcasting). You'll need a fairly popular show to even make your money back, and unless you want to become a professional podcaster, that may just be taking you away from what you do best.

I was on the fence about bringing on sponsors to my own show, the "Agents of Change" podcast. I wanted to start generating income from my podcast, which was averaging about 10,000 downloads a month. Based on those numbers, I only would have made $100-$200 each month, and I would have had to include a 30-second, a 60-second, and another 30-second sponsor message in each show.

I just didn't feel it was worth it.

While I was hemming and hawing over this, one of my listeners posted a link to a recent episode about website conversions on his Twitter account along with the message, "We could use help on this!"

I tweeted him back, which led to some direct messages, then emails, and finally a phone call. In the end, he ended up hiring flyte for a six-month engagement that was worth over twenty-thousand dollars! At the time of this writing it's been extended to over $40,000 of revenue for flyte.

I'm not sharing this story to brag (seriously!), but rather to point out that your podcast can be a great source of leads for your business.

How to Get Started with Podcasting

Most of the successful, passionate podcasters I know are avid podcast *listeners*. If you haven't listened to a podcast, I recommend that as your first step.

Visit iTunes or Stitcher radio and do a search for podcasts in your niche. In iTunes it's easy to see which are the most popular shows in a category. Download and subscribe to a few of these.

It's also a good idea to listen to shows from other categories to get new ideas. When I first started my podcast, I downloaded the most popular show in every category to see how other people were doing their shows.

Podcasts tend to fall into three types of shows:

- Solo: this is more like a lecture or presentation. It often requires a lot work, but you get to establish yourself as the expert.

- Interview: you interview guests who come on your show. You have to share the spotlight, but it's a lot less prep work on your part, and you benefit from the expertise of others. (This is the style of my own show.)
- Panel: a cast of regulars weigh in on topics. Sort of like *Meet the Press* or ESPN's *Around the Horn*. Sometimes the panel rotates with new people, but usually there's a core group.

Of course, you don't have to have just one style. Most of my episodes are interviews, but I'll occasionally do a solo episode to mix it up.

Being a Guest

One way to get your feet wet in podcasting without jumping into the deep end is being a guest on other people's podcasts.

Being a guest is a lot less work than having your own show. You just need to show up on time, do your 20-40 minutes of answering questions, and be on your way. For this investment in time you are introduced to your host's audience and generally will get at least one inbound link from their show notes to your website.

To find an appropriate show to appear on, head on over to iTunes and do a search on your area of expertise. Chances are there are already a number of podcasts that speak to your audience. Find ones that are interview style (meaning they're looking for guests) and listen to a couple of episodes. If it feels like a good fit, find the host's contact information (often on their website), and reach out.

Explain why you'd be a good guest. Give some examples of topics you could speak on where you have some expertise. If you have any previous interview experience you can include links where they can check you out. If you haven't been on any other podcasts, you might send them a clip of you speaking from a YouTube video. If you don't have that, considering creating a brief, two-minute video so they can get a sense of who you are and upload it to YouTube.

Hosts are often looking for people they know will be good guests, so make sure you have something you can point them to, and be clear about the value you'd bring to their audience.

When searching for podcasts, don't *just* look for podcasts in your direct niche. For example, if you're in Public Relations, other PR podcasters may not be interested in having a "competitor" on their show. However, if your firm focuses on the hospitality industry, you should find podcasts that have an audience of innkeepers, restauranteurs, and other professionals in the hospitality industry that could benefit from some positive PR.

Being a Great Guest

If you really want to nail your guest spot, you'll want to prepare.

Listen to a few episodes.

You should have done this before reaching out, but if you find yourself in this situation, make sure you listen to a few episodes before going on the show to get a sense of the host's style. Some hosts send out frameworks for the show, others send the questions in advance, but others are more laid back and just want to see where the conversation goes.

Have a microphone.

You want to sound GREAT on your interview, so speaking into your computer mic just isn't going to cut it. I've got some recommendations below, but at a minimum you want a USB headset. You can pick one up at Amazon or a local store for under $30.

Most interviews I've been on are done on Skype, although some shows prefer Google Hangouts or GoToMeeting. Regardless, most are recorded on a computer, so you'll want that USB powered headset.

Be prepared and show up on time.

Ask the host (if he doesn't tell you in advance) how the show will be recorded. Audio only or video, too? (You don't want to roll out of bed or have a stained shirt on only to find out you're going to be on camera.)

Does he mind if you promote a new product or service? Can you provide a giveaway for his audience?

Show up on time! I can't believe how many times I've shown up for an interview and the guest or host isn't around!

Assuming you can give his audience a freebie, do it. Whether it's a download, an assessment, or a discount in your store, provide it at your website with a nod to his show. For example, if you are on Pat Flynn's *Smart Passive Income* podcast, you might offer a free download that is available at *www.mywebsite.com/spi*. That makes it feel more exclusive, even if it's the same download you offer to every podcast you're on.

You can put that download or discount behind an email registration or just make it available to any listener, depending on your goals.

Recording Equipment & Software

One of the questions that most people have when they want to start podcasting is around equipment and software. Which on some level is the *least* important piece of the puzzle, because there are so many excellent solutions out there.

But to put your mind at rest, I'll share what you'll need and what I use for each of those categories. And because most people who podcast for a living have their own favorite set of tools, I'll link to their lists of recommended hardware and software as well.

Keep in mind that you can start inexpensively and then upgrade over time. Most podcasters *don't* start by dropping several thousand dollars on equipment.

Microphone

You never want to use the internal mic on your computer. While it may be able to record your voice, it's going to sound tinny and far away. Lots of people will listen to your show while driving, possibly with the windows down, so the quality of your voice is paramount.

For years I used a **Sennheiser PC-36** headset. It was under $30 on Amazon. Recently it broke and I was less thrilled with the newer version of it, so I purchased the **Blue Microphones Yeti USB Microphone**, which is a standalone mic as opposed to a headset. I also added a **DragonPad** filter that keeps my "p's" from popping. That setup was less than $150.

Recording Software

Since most of my podcasts are interviews, I've found that **Skype** is the best tool for hosting the interviews, and **Call Recorder**, a $30 Skype plugin, is the right tool for recording those interviews.

What I like about Call Recorder is that it records both sides of the conversation as individual tracks. This is true for both audio and video. If one of us is significantly louder than the other, it can easily be fixed in post-production.

Mixer

I don't use a mixer in my current setup. Many professional podcasters that do like the **Firestudio Project** by Presonus.

Audio Editing Software

I'm on a Mac and I've found that **GarageBand** is all I need to get the job done. Some other people prefer **Audition** or **Audacity**.

ID3 Editor

Once you've got your podcast recording completed, you'll want to add some additional information to the file. This is where an ID3 Editor comes in. It allows you to add information to fields such as:

- Title
- Description
- Copyright
- Podcast art
- Artist (host)

and more.

The one I use is simply called **ID3 Editor**. (No points for creativity.)

Hosting

Almost all podcasters I know use **Libsyn** for their podcast hosting. It's a great, affordable service that handles most of the heavy lifting for you. Accounts start at $5/month, but for some of the detailed statistics, you'll want to spend $15 or more a month. As you get more listeners, you may also need to pay more.

Libsyn makes it easy to push your new episodes out to services like iTunes and Stitcher Radio.

Website

If you're creating a podcast to build your business, you'll want a website where you can send people for show notes, links you mentioned in the show, and other lead magnets. While you can do this on most platforms, I prefer WordPress and the **Blubrry PowerPress** plugin for podcasting.

Second Opinions

If you'd like to see what some of the leaders in business podcasts are using as far as equipment goes, I've created links to their equipment pages here:

http://theleadmachinebook.com/podcast

Polishing Your Podcast

As you can see, although there are a few moving pieces, anyone can get started in podcasting these days for very little investment. Another way of looking at it is that there's a lot of competition out there!

To make your podcast stand out, you'll want to add some professional polish to the show. Hopefully listening to some other podcasts has given you some ideas of things you like that you can adopt for your own show.

Podcast Art

You may not be able to judge a book by its cover, but when someone is cruising through iTunes, an eye-catching graphic will make them more likely to take a chance on your show.

Apple currently recommends podcast art at 1,400 x 1,400 pixels. You can probably find a local designer to create the graphic or head on over to Fiverr.com and look for "podcast cover art."

Voiceover

Having another voice on the podcast, introducing you and the show, and potentially introducing different segments on the show, makes you sound bigger than you (currently) are. Voice actors can be found easily on Fiverr.com, or you can hire local talent to record a few intros and outros.

Royalty-Free Music

You're probably *not* going to have an original score or theme song written for you when you first launch your podcast, but that doesn't mean you can't find music that fits the vibe of your show. Just like there's royalty-free photography, there's royalty-free music, too. Often at the same sites.

Just Google "royalty free music" for websites that specialize in these offerings.

When I first launched my podcast it was called "The Marketing Agents Podcast" and had an old, adventure serial feel to it. I searched for "Indiana Jones" on a royalty-free music site and found musical scores that were just different enough so they wouldn't get anyone in hot water, while still providing the feel of an old-timey adventure.

When I rebranded as The "Agents of Change" podcast, I wanted more of a spy vibe, so I searched on "Mission: Impossible," "The Man from UNCLE," and "James Bond" before finding the perfect music to set the tone.

As with all social media, the more you brand your podcast, the more it helps it stand out from your competitors who aren't putting in the same level of effort.

Giving Good Interview

I enjoy the interview podcast, as a listener, as a guest, and as a host. It's great to get different opinions, hear different voices, and the Q&A format is something we all understand.

I've heard from both my guests and my audience that I "give good interview." This could just be the "Ugly Baby Syndrome," where the people who think you have an ugly baby aren't going to tell you. But I got some great advice from Michael Stelzner before I started, so let's assume they're telling me the truth. Here's what I do:

Get good guests.

We've all had turkeys on our podcast. People that made us want to stop the interview halfway through, or we just didn't want to publish their episode.

To avoid this, it's a good idea to vet them first.

I've found that people who have their own podcast are almost always good guests, too. They know the format, they have good equipment, and they know how to make a host look good. Still, you should listen to an episode or two of their shows first.

Professional speakers are *often* good guests, but many of them are more used to speaking without being interrupted by questions, so I've had some bad experiences, too. Be prepared to occasionally interrupt them with questions like, "Let me make sure I understand what you're saying," and, "How exactly does that work?"

You want them to speak, but you also want to create some structure around the show.

Another place to get good guests is from influencer lists. Almost every industry has annual lists of the biggest influencers. Just Google "[year] + [industry] + influencer" to see who's out there for you to interview. These people also bring big audiences with them, so they may promote your show to their audience as well.

Ask the right questions.

Often the first question is about the interviewee's origin story. This is a helpful question if the guest is relatively unknown, especially to your audience. However, if you have landed someone who does a lot of interviews, or is well known to your audience, this may be unnecessary, or even frustrating to the guest who has had to answer this question in a hundred other interviews.

I have a few favorite questions that tend to get good responses. Let's take a look.

The "Defend Your Position" Question:

This question is phrased along the lines that a lot of our listeners may think your process won't work, can't be done, is too much work, won't have the ROI they need, etc. "What would you say to these people?"

The "How Do We Get Started" Question:

After the guest has "won me over" with her arguments on why this is important and worthwhile, I will ask how we get started, especially if we're "starting from scratch" or "don't yet have an audience." I like this question because often the starting point is so far in the guest's rear view mirror that they forget to talk about this.

The "Biggest Mistakes" Question:

Simply put, these are the mistakes that people might make when building an email list, training their dog, or opening a pizzeria.

The "If There Was One Thing" Question:

This is similar to the biggest mistakes question, but it also gets to the heart of one thing that could really derail your audience from success: "If there was one thing you know now that you didn't know when you first started investing/alligator wrestling/competitive eating, what would it be?"

The "Where Can We Find You Online" Question:

I always wrap with an opportunity for the guest to drive traffic to his website, squeeze page, or anywhere else he'd like to send his audience.

Summarize the guest's points.

Even the best guest can get off point or go off on a tangent. I often take notes during the interview, especially if my guest is going through her signature "Four-step process for running Facebook ads that convert."

When she's done, I'll often read them back to her, "To make sure I got them down right."

Or, if someone's been talking for quite some time, I'll often gently break into the monologue to "Make sure I understand what you're saying."

I've received several unsolicited emails from listeners that this "recap" was the most valuable piece of the entire interview. You may not need to do this with every guest...some are excellent in giving soundbites to your audience...however, it can be a powerful tool.

My Podcast Workflow

Although my process for creating a podcast has changed over time, let me share with you how I currently manage my show.

Find a guest.

I started as most people do, with the people I knew and trusted. After that, I started checking out other podcasters who had shows that complimented my own. I'd also listen to other, similar podcasts and find guests I liked, or wanted to know more from.

I also started to look through influencer lists. Or if I wanted to get someone for a specific topic, say "Twitter ads" or "online reputation," I'd tap my network to see who was the expert in the field. And as my show gained traction, I found that people were seeking me out get on my show.

Schedule a time.

I use the calendar app TimeTrade to have guests find a time that works for them. There are a number of similar apps out there, so find one that works for you. These apps are great because they cut down on the inevitable back and forth emails about when people are available...only to find out you're in different time zones and you have to start from scratch!

You just block out the times on your personal calendar that don't work for you, or you want to keep sacred to get work done, and the guest only sees the times that work.

In these apps you can also include information like that you'll need a short bio and a head shot, that they should have a microphone, that it's audio only (or video), and so on.

Prep.

Some hosts like to go into their interviews cold so they can ask the questions their audience would ask. Others read every blog, listen to every podcast, and devour every book the interviewee has ever written.

I like to have ten or so questions ready to go as a framework for the show, but if I find something interesting in one of the answers that I wasn't expecting, I'll often follow it down the rabbit hole. You need to find your own level of preparedness.

If I'm interviewing someone I've never spoken to before, I often see if they want to set up a pre-interview chat so we can talk through the ideas in the show. This makes the interview flow better, and improves our banter.

I also share who our audience is, because good guests want to tailor their conversation to fit the audience. They may normally focus on corporations, but if they know they're speaking to small business owners, they can pivot or come up with more relevant examples.

Some shows have a show flow that they send to the guests. Some shows have the same questions for every guest. There's no wrong way to do it.

I tend not to send my guests the questions first. I prefer more of a conversational tone. If I am really a beginner on a subject, I may ask the guest for a few questions to get started, or some type of framework to make for a better show. After all, I want us both to look good!

The day before or the day of I make sure that we're connected on Skype and send them a reminder of our interview time. I'll also confirm that I have a short bio and head shot.

The interview.

Once I get someone on Skype I'll usually chat them up for a few minutes first, like warming up in the on deck circle. It also gives me a chance to check the quality of their audio.

I'll tell or remind them about how long we'll go, that I'll give them a chance to pitch their book or website at the end, and that we'll provide links in the show notes. I tell them to hang on after we "hang up" so we can debrief.

Before we start I make sure I am pronouncing their name correctly. Then I click the record button on Call Recorder and we're off to the races!

The transcript.

Most people go with show notes...just the highlights of the show. I prefer a full transcript. This is because not everyone loves, understands, or has the time for podcasts. I've had a few clients who I've sent a link for a podcast that I felt would be beneficial to them, and they tell me later that they read the transcript instead.

For about $20 an episode, I can reach a wider audience. You can certainly find transcriptionists for less, but my transcriptionist also finds a great sound clip from our guest to start the show with, finds the best quote for the graphic we create for each show, comes up with potential episode titles, and tracks down all the links, even ones we hadn't thought of.

(Seriously, she's great. If you want her contact info hit me up on Twitter at @therichbrooks.)

Intro/outro.

I record a separate intro and outro for each show afterward. In the intro I usually tease the content, talk about some other things that are going on, and maybe share a little personal nugget.

In the outro I remind people of the show notes, give them the URL where they can check them out, maybe ask for a review on iTunes or to tell a friend, and sign off.

Editing.

When I started, I did all my own editing, but now I have a team member at flyte handle that for me. Using GarageBand, the order goes like this:

- **Audio Quote:** The :15-:45 second clip from my guest that my transcriptionist found for us to get people excited about the show content.
- **Music:** Our *Mission: Impossible* inspired audio comes in and fades into...
- **Narrator Intro:** I had my brother's father-in-law record three intros, three outros, and some other audio clips to make the show sound more professional. We rotate these each week for variety. Oh, and my brother's father-in-law was the entertainment reporter for ABC Radio for like fifty years, in case you were wondering why I chose him.
- **My Intro**
- **Interview**
- **My Outro**
- **Narrator Outro**
- **Closing Music**

Sometimes we have other segments, so I'll record some extra audio to introduce them.

If you don't want to do this yourself—it's time consuming! — and you don't have co-workers who can help you out, there are virtual assistants or podcast service providers who can do it for you.

In fact, they can do the editing, tagging, uploading, and just about anything else you want to outsource.

Tagging.

The next task is to tag the audio file with additional meta information. This is also a task I now outsource.

Upload to Libsyn.

The tagged file is then uploaded to Libsyn, our podcast hosting company. We fill out the title, description, and when we want the file available to our listeners.

Post show notes.

The full transcript, along with some introductory text, is then posted to our blog. We use the PowerPress plugin to make the audio playable from the post.

My team also creates two images of our guest, a favorite quote from the interview, and our branding. One is horizontal, for Facebook and Twitter, the other is vertical for Pinterest. If you look at the post, you'll only see the vertical version at the top of the page. We hide the other one, but using something called Open Graph Protocol Settings, we're able to set the horizontal image as the image to be shared on Facebook. We do this because we want the post to look as professional and inviting as possible when people share it on their favorite social network.

Actually, we create a third version of the image, which is bigger, for the slideshow on the home page of the site. We really want to drive traffic to our new interviews!

Once this is all done, we hit publish and review the post one final time to make sure it looks good.

Share the post.

Once it's live, I share the post across all the social channels by clicking on the share buttons at the top of the post. We don't want any goose eggs up there.

Links from other pages.

Once we have the post (and show) live, I find other, more established, pages on our websites where I can create inbound links to this post.

Email interviewee.

We then send an email to the guest, letting him or her know the show is live. We include a link to the post with the show and the show notes, as well as a link to iTunes and Stitcher Radio.

I also include an embed code in case they want to use the interview on their own blog. Ted Rubin asked me for that one time and it became one of my most popular episodes because of his audience.

Also, since we went through all the trouble of creating a cool looking graphic featuring them, I put that in the email, too.

I don't explicitly ask guests to share the podcast, although I certainly hope they do. I've been asked by hosts when I'm the guest in the past to share with my audience, and sometimes it comes off as too aggressive or desperate.

Choose your own adventure here.

Email my list.

Nothing drives traffic like email. Sure, you'll have a lot of your listening audience subscribed through iTunes or Stitcher, but for those don't like those services, or don't check them often enough, email is a great way of getting more downloads.

Growing Your Podcast Audience

Like most platforms, you're using your podcast to amplify your reach. So how do you reach more of your intended audience?

Get Found in iTunes

Although algorithms constantly change, there are specific places that you should focus your attention when it comes to getting found in an iTunes search.

- Your show title
- The host
- Your episode title

At this point, the iTunes search is not as *nuanced* as the Google search, so feel free to over-optimize your titles and host.

For example, Pat Flynn's *Smart Passive Income* podcast becomes *"The Smart Passive Income Podcast: Online Business | Blogging | Passive Income | Pat Flynn"* and the host is *"Pat Flynn: Online Entrepreneur, Business Strategist and Blogger."*

Go on Other Shows

The great thing about other shows' audiences is that they already listen to podcasts! By making time to be a guest on other relevant shows, you are getting in front of your type of audience.

Push Your Audience to Subscribe

One of the other metrics iTunes looks at is new subscribers. While many of your listeners may already be subscribed, not all of them are, so mention this at the end of your episodes. Explain the benefits.

Final Thoughts on Podcasting

While podcasting may not be as accessible or popular as some other platforms like blogs and video, it does offer real value.

Many of your ideal clients are auditory learners, so they can connect with you while they're doing other things like driving a car or mowing the lawn. The medium is intimate, as you often speak directly into their ears. Your audience will feel like they know you, which helps build trust.

It's also a great platform to connect with influencers who might not normally give you the time of day, but have no problem being a guest on your show.

Finally, if you have some help—either from co-workers or a VA (virtual assistant)—podcasting can be a very time-efficient way to create content. The production, post-production, and promotion of the show are all time-consuming efforts that can be outsourced.

YouTube

There are plenty of places to host your videos online, but when it comes to marketing reach, Nothing Compares 2 U... YouTube that is.

Your Audience Is Watching

Over one billion people use YouTube monthly, putting it only behind Facebook in terms of reach. Every day, four billion videos are watched. Every day, one billion videos are watched on a mobile device.

When it comes to Internet users, in the US, 43% of baby boomers use YouTube. 58% of U.S. Generation X. 81% of millennials. 81.9% of teens.

Yet only 9% of small businesses use YouTube to reach their ideal customers. Talk about an opportunity for you!

YouTube is Great for SEO

You may have heard that YouTube is the second most popular search engine in the world, only behind Google, its parent company.

Undoubtedly, you've done a Google search and seen YouTube videos as the top results. In fact, I often tell people that if your competition is entrenched in the top organic listings in Google, but they don't do video, YouTube is your best chance at leapfrogging them in the results.

YouTube is often a direct destination for people who want to search on a solution...everything from "How to Serve an Ace in

Tennis" to "How to Get Up on a Wakeboard" to "How to Study for a Pop Quiz."

If you're looking to get in front of your ideal customer while they're in a moment of need, YouTube can help.

YouTube is Great for Engagement

Video is as close as you can get online to talking to your clients in real life. They can see your passion, hear your voice, and watch for other non-verbal communications.

You can reach them on their desktop or smartphone.

You can get them to subscribe to your YouTube channel so they are alerted to new videos you post.

You can drive the traffic from the video page or even from within the video itself to your website or opt-in page.

For all these reasons and more, you should consider adding YouTube to your lead generation efforts.

Making Your Videos

For the small businesses that *are* using YouTube, many of them aren't doing a very good job of creating engaging videos.

They're posting their own TV commercials, an interview with one of the founders that ran on a local talk show, or a video with so little production value that it actually damages the brand. None of these are going to attract or engage an audience.

What should I make my videos about?

If lead generation is your goal, I want you to think about YouTube videos like you would blog posts. Each one needs to provide value to your ideal customer when they're in a moment of distress. When they need help. When they are acutely aware of their pain point.

Each video needs to be optimized for the search engines just a blog post would be. It needs to have a tight focus, consideration to a specific keyword, and include a call to action.

And just as no one blog post will generate enough business for you, you shouldn't think that one video will, either. Create videos that support your most important lines of business.

So, begin by doing your keyword research, just like you did for your website and blog. The only additional tool I might consider here is the YouTube autocomplete search feature. By going to YouTube and beginning a relevant search, you can find other, related searches that may inspire you to explore new topics.

Have a cooking product? Type "how to cook" in the search box and let YouTube make some suggestions. Run a snowboarding school? Try "snowboarding how-to" and see all the things people most want to learn. Are you a professional organizer? The "how to organize" search will give you tons of ideas of which videos you should work on first.

How do I create videos?

These days, we all have video cameras in our computers and our phones, so the ability to create videos is already at our fingertips. For those people who want to look better than the competition, you can certainly invest in a stand-alone video camera, tripod, lights and more.

If your video is going to be mostly a screen recording—like I do with my how-to digital marketing videos—then you may want to pick up a copy of ScreenFlow (Mac) or Camtasia (Mac or Windows.) This also works well if you don't want to appear on camera yourself. You can create a slideshow and just do voiceovers.

Once the video has been created, you can use a video editor like iMovie or the two screen capture tools mentioned above. You can also use a more professional tool like Adobe Premiere or Apple's Final Cut Pro.

There are also plenty of local videographers who can help you create high-quality videos affordably. And if my definition of affordably doesn't match yours, there's often a university or community college that is looking to place interns.

Uploading Your Videos to YouTube

Uploading your videos to YouTube requires a YouTube account, also called a "channel." Since YouTube is owned by Google, this account is often tied to other Google products. However, Google keeps changing its products and rules, so it's hard to know what—if any—rules will be in effect when you go to set up your channel.

If you already have a Google account that you're using strictly for your business, where you set up your Google Analytics, Search Console, or Adwords, I'd recommend using that same account for YouTube as well. However, you should look for a channel name that represents you best. That might mean your company name, or it might mean what you do and where you're from.

Like all social media outposts, I recommend that you brand your YouTube channel as much as you can. That includes your username, vanity URL, profile picture, and header image. The more you customize it, the more branding equity you get and the more credibility you gain.

Once you have your channel set up, you'll want to upload your first video. YouTube often plays with features to provide a better overall experience, so if something doesn't line up exactly with what I list below, roll with the punches. These are the desktop instructions; while you can upload video from your phone, a lot of these tasks are easier when you have a full keyboard in front of you.

- **Rename your video file.** Many videos are uploaded with the original file names like L4K3993.MOV. One thing YouTube looks at in their search algorithm is the file name, so before you even upload your video, give it a keyword rich title like "Best Drones Under 100 Dollars.mov."

- **Click the Upload button.** It's often found at the top of your YouTube home page when you're logged in. It will take you to a page where you can drag and drop your video or click an upload button and navigate to it on your computer.

- **Mark the video as unlisted.** Optional. I do this because I like playing around with my video a bit before I unveil it to the world.

- **Begin the upload and add metadata.** Once the video has begun uploading, YouTube gives you the opportunity to add additional information, similar to what you did with the ID3 tags on your podcast.
  - **Title**: As with a blog post, the title may be the most important element in YouTube's search. Make sure it's keyword rich and the best keywords come at the beginning of your title.
  - **Description:** Many entrepreneurs put in no description or just a short description. You can put up to 2,000 characters here, so use them! You can include links to your website, which can drive traffic. You just need to specify the full URL, like this: http://www.mycompany.com/product-page for the link to work. Consider putting the URL first, as well as at the bottom of your description.
  - **Tags:** Put all relevant keywords here. Include branded keywords like your company or product names, too, as this can help you in "related" searches.
  - **Additional fields:** You may find some additional fields. Complete them as you see fit.

Creating Calls to Action

There are a few ways in which you can create calls to action with your videos. YouTube allows us to create CTAs for both activities that take place in YouTube (subscribe to a channel, watch another video, watch a playlist of videos, etc.) or outside YouTube (driving traffic to your website).

Although getting subscribers to your YouTube channel can help your ranking in YouTube search, and offering multiple videos to watch can help you engage a prospect, I'm going to focus on getting viewers off YouTube and onto your website or squeeze page.

Any of the CTAs below will work better if you include a verbal CTA to go along with it. For example, let's say you've created a video about all the medical shots a viewer needs if they plan on traveling the world. As your lead magnet, back on your website, you've provided a checklist of these vaccines and whether they're readily available.

During the video, you might say, "for a printable checklist of all these vaccines, please visit the link in the description / please click the button on the screen." That verbal direction can make all the difference in getting someone to take an action.

Description CTAs

A link in your description is the simplest way to create a clickable link to your website. However, the link must be spelled out with the http:// prefix, otherwise it won't work. So there's no way to have a clickable, keyword rich link that's not a full URL.

Also, if your video is embedded somewhere, say a blog post or Facebook, the description won't appear, so the link is not going to appear either.

I recommend starting your description with the link so that it's guaranteed to show, even when YouTube is only showing the first two lines of your description.

Depending on how long your description is, you might repeat that link at the bottom of the description or a few times throughout the text.

Annotations

Annotations allow you to add clickable links and buttons right into your YouTube videos! These links can even link to your website or squeeze page. Unlike Description CTAs, these remain in your video even when it's embedded somewhere else.

Now, creating annotations is a little bit trickier than creating a simple link in the Description, but it's worth it. And it's not like you need to learn any code. You just log into your YouTube account, choose to edit a video, and then choose to add annotations.

Currently, YouTube will only allow you to create links to an approved, verified site. However, once you've gotten your website approved, you can use a plugin like Pretty Link to redirect the traffic from your site to a specific page offsite. This is helpful if you want to link to your book on Amazon or your art on Etsy, for example.

Setting up annotations is simple once you've done it a few times, but YouTube is often moving things around. I've created a couple of helpful how-to videos if you'd like to watch a step-by-step tutorial on annotations.

http://theleadmachinebook.com/annotations

The only downside of annotations is that they don't work on mobile devices!

Cards

YouTube Cards allow you to create visual, in-video CTAs that also work on mobile devices. With so many people watching videos on a mobile device, this may be the best way forward. The only downside is that it feels a little limiting in terms of creative, but that might be a worthwhile tradeoff to generate leads from your customers on mobile devices.

As with annotations, it might be easier to see how these are set up rather than try to read about them. You can check out some tutorials here:

http://theleadmachinebook.com/cards

Getting More Viewers

While quality always trumps quantity, there's no doubt that getting more qualified viewers is better than getting fewer qualified viewers. To that end, let's talk about how you can get more eyeballs on your video.

Optimize your video for search. If you followed the instructions above, then you can check this off your list.

Embed your video in a blog post. All YouTube videos come with an embed code. By adding the embed code to your blog post you can share your video with your blog readers as well. You can further optimize the post for increased search traffic by writing a blog post that's related to the copy, or by simply using a transcript of the video.

Share your video on social media. Right under your video are some social share buttons. You can use these or post the YouTube URL directly in your social media updates.

Email your list. One thing YouTube is looking for is a surge of views. Promoting your video to your opt-in list of subscribers can drive a lot more traffic than social alone.

Get engagement. YouTube is also looking for engagement from your visitors. It's OK to ask people to like your video, leave a comment, or subscribe to your channel. If the most popular channels on YouTube are asking for engagement, you should, too!

Other Video Sites

While there are other sites that host video, I've never found any that equal YouTube in terms of audience reach, cost, or breadth of marketing tools.

The only other site I use for video hosting is Vimeo. Businesses will want Vimeo Pro, which currently costs about two hundred dollars a year. What I like about Vimeo is the quality of the video that's been uploaded and the control I have over who gets to see it.

When I want a marketing video, I go to YouTube. When I want more control over my video, like when we post the Agents of Change Digital Marketing Conference videos for Virtual Pass holders only, Vimeo is our go-to solution.

Takeaways

YouTube offers you a way to reach and engage a large audience. It can help with SEO and driving traffic to your website.

Think of your videos like visual blog posts. Optimize them for search, create value for your viewers, and include a call to action.

Using annotations and cards on your videos, you can drive viewers back to your website. With the offer of an irresistible lead magnet that ties into your video, you can build your email list.

SlideShare

SlideShare, owned by LinkedIn, may not be the most well-known platform out there, but it does boast 70 million users. (Boasting may be the appropriate phrase here: there's no mention of how active these 70 million users are, or how one qualifies as a "user" of the service.)

In any case, SlideShare is rarely the first social platform that any marketer or small business will use. However, it can still provide a great way of reaching, engaging, and converting your ideal customer.

If you've never been to SlideShare, it's like YouTube for PowerPoint presentations. You create a slide deck, upload it, and add meta-data just like you do on YouTube. You can share the link to your deck through nearby social sharing buttons. People can click through each slide, and you can even add audio or video to your deck. People can like, share, and comment on your decks.

You can even embed your slide deck in other places like your blog...just like YouTube.

Also, if there are any links in your slide deck, they will (usually) be there in the uploaded version as well. That means you can include CTAs within your slides that drive traffic to a specific page on your site.

While SlideShare is primarily for a B2B audience, there's no rule that would keep a creative B2C company from uploading a slide deck and taking advantage of the tools, audience, and metrics of SlideShare.

How to Make the Most of SlideShare

For some, SlideShare is a free online tool that makes converting a slide deck into an interactive, online experience a snap. For others, it's about getting in front of a wider audience. Still others use it as a way of repurposing and repackaging content.

Below are a few ways in which you can make the most of this "sleeping giant" of social media platforms.

Get more bang for your buck from presentations.

Simply put, if you're putting on presentations for marketing purposes, you can take your slide deck and upload it to Slide-Share. You'll get more eyeballs on your content for a minimum amount of work on your end.

Although it's certainly not going to be as engaging as seeing you present live, it may introduce new people to your work.

Repurpose blog posts.

This works especially well for list posts. When I ran The Marketing Agents blog, we had a lot of list posts, such as *13 Facebook Marketing Tips for Small Business*.

I had designed a slide deck template for The Marketing Agents brand, and had someone from my office turn each tip into its own slide. Along with an intro and closing slide, the deck was only 15 slides long. However, that deck got viewed over 1,000 times since it was uploaded with zero additional promotion from me and 15 minutes of work from my co-worker.

That's a solid investment!

Create a fresh deck.

If you really want to invest a little extra effort in SlideShare, consider creating a brand new deck based around a topic. The decks that do best on SlideShare tend to be longer decks that have obviously been crafted specifically for SlideShare.

This is because each slide is self-explanatory and any appropriate text appears on the slide itself. (During live presentations, minimal text should appear on a slide, as the slide should not be competing with the speaker.) These decks are often 75 or more slides long. They're more like slideshows than traditional decks.

Embed decks in new blog posts.

Assuming you didn't just create a deck from a blog post (or at least not one from the same blog), you can embed your Slide-Share deck right into your blog as if it were a YouTube video. Like the YouTube example from the previous chapter, you should include contextual copy so that the search engines understand what the post is all about.

You can also embed other people's decks in your own blog post. While this might seem counter-intuitive, many sites attract a lot of visitors by artfully showcasing other people's work.

Add decks to your LinkedIn profile.

Since SlideShare is owned by LinkedIn, it's easy to add these decks to your profile. When you're looking at your own uploads, you'll see the ability to quickly add a deck to your post.

Lead Generation on SlideShare

SlideShare runs on a "freemium model," much like LinkedIn. Many tools are free, but some cost extra. Recently, SlideShare started giving away most of their ProTools for free. However, the ability to capture emails within the slide deck wasn't one of them.

If you want to capture emails or generate leads from SlideShare, you'll either need to upgrade to the Paid Enterprise level, or rely on CTAs and links to your squeeze page from within the slide deck itself.

Webinars

I know what you're thinking. "Webinars are *not* social media."

I would disagree. I believe they can be made social...they don't need to be one-directional sales tools that cause people to tune out. Instead, they can be engaging and get people excited about participation.

One of the things that makes webinars a great platform for your message is that most people now understand the concept: It's a presentation I can attend in my underwear. Unless I work in a cubicle.

Because that would be weird.

When people sign up for your webinar, they are providing you with their contact information. There is an implicit agreement that they have now joined your mailing list. If you feel like making that message a little more explicit, you can let them know that, too.

In fact, webinars are currently one of the most popular methods of growing an email list and warming leads. They work great for information products, but they can also be used for services and physical products as well.

Some marketers prefer live webinars while others like to have a library of on-demand content available. There's no wrong answer here, and you can certainly record live webinars and turn them into on-demand content down the line.

What should my webinar be about?

Again, webinars are just another delivery system where you can provide value for your clients, customers, and prospects. A virtual venue where you can establish your credibility, demonstrate your expertise, and build trust with people.

The topic of your webinar should be based on what your ideal customer is suffering from (and what you can help them with).

- A commercial realtor might put on a webinar on the paperwork and approval process for first time buyers of commercial real estate.
- A web design firm may put on a webinar about how business owners can measure the effectiveness of their websites.
- A college entry consultant could put on a webinar about how to prepare for an interview with a reach school.

If you've been listening to your customers and have done your keyword research, coming up with ideas for your webinars should be no problem at all.

If you're still struggling for ideas, Google your ideal customer or their problem and add "webinar" to your search.

- New food truck owner *webinar*
- Reality show audition tape *webinar*
- Permaculture design *webinar*

How to Promote Your Webinar

True story: I once had a guy show up to our office and announce he was there for the webinar. Luckily, his office was only a five-minute walk away, so we told him to go home.

I bring that up because webinars don't tend to attract a lot of "walk-in" traffic, and no one's going to accidentally stumble into your webinar. You'll have to promote it.

One of the first questions you need to answer, who are you trying to reach? If you're focused on building your list and acquiring new leads, you may not want to bother emailing your list. On the other hand, if you're trying to warm leads, build trust, or educate your current customers for the possibility of upselling them, then it makes sense to email your list.

For live events, you'll need to heavily promote the webinar, primarily through social media and digital ads, and email marketing if appropriate. You'll want to get people in "seats."

For on-demand content, you can promote it the same way, but since it's not as time-sensitive, you can also use SEO to drive traffic.

For a lot of marketers, advertising on Facebook is a popular tactic. It allows you to narrowly target your ideal customer and drive them to an opt-in page. We'll look at the details of Facebook marketing and the different tactics you can employ when we get to the Digital Advertising section.

You can also advertise on Google, Twitter, Pinterest, Instagram, or LinkedIn, although LinkedIn advertising costs tend to be higher than the other platforms, and by my own experience, as well as the experience of others I've discussed this with, it provides a lower ROI. YMMV. (Your mileage may vary.)

One thing I've noticed is that if you plan on putting on a webinar about how to use a specific platform, that platform is often a great place to advertise, because your ideal customer is already there.

You can promote your webinar through social media updates, blog posts, YouTube videos and even your podcast. Remember that different members of your audience are used to interacting with you on different platforms, so be sure to talk up your webinar wherever they hang out.

You can also promote your webinar by creating a Facebook Event and inviting people to the event. You can promote it on an events page on your website, on your home page, or on the sidebar of your blog.

The goal of all of these promotional tactics are to drive people to your opt-in page for your webinar.

Choosing a Webinar Platform

There are a number of platforms you can use to put on your webinar such as Google Hangouts, Skype, WebEx, and WebinarJam, to name a few. Personally, I use GoToWebinar and it's always worked well for me.

It works on all modern browsers, it has just the right amount of built-in tools, it's very dependable, it's got great signup tools, and it has tiered pricing depending on your needs. You may find that one of the other platforms may be a better fit for your personal needs, but you can't go wrong with GoToWebinar.

Tips for Putting on a Good Webinar

Webinars can often be dry, boring affairs, where your audience is barely listening to you as they also check emails, surf the web, or take a call while you're speaking. You want to get them engaged as much as possible. Here are some tips for improving the quality of your webinars:

Let everyone know you're showing up 10-15 minutes early if they want to chat with you beforehand. I'll often ask people their name, where they're from, what they hope to learn, etc. During this pre-Q & A you can start to build rapport with your audience.

You'll want to have a decent mic so that you sound good while you're speaking. You definitely don't want to be using the default mic on your laptop. If people struggle to hear you, they'll tune out.

You'll want to have some recording software. GoToWebinar has a built in recording option, or you can use a third party tool. People always ask if the webinar is going to be recorded. This is code for: Do I really need to show up?

Some marketers won't provide a recording because they want people there live. Others will offer one. Still others say they're not sure, and recommend that people show up live because sometimes things go wrong with the recording. Whatever path you take, make sure you tell people that the only way to see the event live or on-demand is by signing up. (And make sure your signup mentions that registrants will be added to your email list.)

If you're planning on showing slides, you'll want to have a tool like PowerPoint or Keynote to create your slide deck. Try to avoid fancy transitions or lots of motion; webinar playback is often choppy and dependent on everyone's connection speed. Better to keep things simple.

It's also a good idea to have more slides in your webinar than you might have in a similar, in-person presentation. This is because you need to keep people's interest, and it's more difficult to do so when two computer screens and the Internet are separating you. More slides mean more things to look at, so there's more engagement.

You can also include breaks in your presentations. You can ask for questions at specific times so that people aren't just sitting back and watching the webinar, they're participating. This keeps engagement high throughout your webinar.

Typically, webinars, especially marketing webinars, are 60-90 minutes long. There's no hard or fast rule about the length, so feel free to try something different.

Once your webinar is over, you can convert the recording into a movie file. You can then turn this into an on-demand webinar that you can either sell or use as a lead magnet for email signups.

Should You Sell on Your Webinar?

Many marketers put on free webinars for the sole purpose of selling people at the end. This is especially true of people who have information products to sell. Others prefer to use the webinar to warm leads and educate customers and prospects. There's no wrong answer here, it just depends on your business goals.

If you've done your job in promoting your webinar, chances are you'll get loads of new email signups anyway. You can segment them in your email list based on the topics you covered. You can also get reports on who attended the webinar and who missed it, so you can send appropriate follow up emails.

Although webinars take place in a hosted environment, such as GoToWebinar, you can certainly follow up via email afterward, driving traffic back to your website. You can also use limited-time offers to spur your audience into action, striking while the iron is hot.

Final Thoughts on Social Platforms

Every business can benefit from social platforms, whether they're on your site like a blog or remote like a YouTube channel or webinar.

They establish your expertise, build your credibility, and provide a home base for your intellectual property.

Also, as you develop out your social networks, they give you something to talk about and promote, driving traffic back to your website or opt-in page.

In short, they're great tools for generating quality leads online.

Next up, we'll look at the other side of social media, social networks.

Facebook

When most people think about social media, they think about Facebook. And with good reason. It's by far the biggest social media platform, with about 1.5 billion *active* users.

Most people I know check in to Facebook at least once a day, and it feels like a few people I know *live* there. That means it's likely that *your* ideal customer is hanging out there, too.

Getting your business on Facebook is free, and you can get people to like your business so they can see your posts, which is also free. You can post pictures, videos, quotes, and more. You can use your status updates to drive traffic to your website or opt-in page.

Facebook also gives you incredible analytics into how people are engaging with your content, showing you what type of content they like, when they want to see it, and how they choose to respond.

What's not to love?!?

What's Not to Love

Only a few years ago, it was easy to reach your fans on Facebook. You would post something and it would show up in their newsfeed more often than not. (The newsfeed is the stream of updates from your friends, the brands you follow, and Sponsored Stories—read: ads—that is constantly being updated. That's where people spend almost all of their time on Facebook.)

Now, for a long time, Facebook has curated the posts you see. Whether you see a post is based on how much you "like" the person or brand behind it, whether the update in question has gotten a lot of engagement already, and a number of other factors.

More recently, Facebook changed its algorithm. Suddenly, businesses that had been getting a lot of visibility disappeared. Now, most business posts are only seen by 1%-5% of their fans! That means for brands that spend a lot of time, energy, and money to build up their fan base, suddenly the value of all those fans dropped dramatically.

Businesses that had put a lot of effort into building their Facebook reach were suddenly left twisting in the wind. Some brands abandoned Facebook altogether. However, Facebook had a solution.

"Pay us."

That's right, through boosted posts, sponsored stories, or ads, you could "pay to play." Some people thought this was outrageous. However, these were the same people who had no problem paying for ads on TV, radio, and in the newspaper.

The good news is that Facebook ads are incredibly powerful, completely measurable, and so far, affordable. (Or at least they provide a positive ROI when you do them right.)

We'll take a closer look at Facebook ads in the next section, but for now I just want to talk about how you can generate more traffic and leads from Facebook organically (without spending money).

The Challenge of Writing about Facebook

There are entire conferences with multiple tracks that last several days just talking about Facebook. That's a lot of information to try and cram into a chapter, or even a book, or even an entire shelf at your locally-owned independent book seller.

Also, there seems to be a seismic change at Facebook every few months. Right now, as I write this chapter, Facebook is heavily promoting live video. If anyone I'm connected to or following uses Facebook Live, I get a notification about it. Facebook is pushing live video *hard*. Right now it makes a lot of sense to be playing around with live video.

Will the same be true by the time you're reading this, or will the newsfeed be oversaturated with live video? Will people be bored with it? Will Facebook be emphasizing something else instead?

For these reasons and more, I'm going to try and focus my attention on some of the more "evergreen" strategies to generate leads from Facebook.

If you want the latest tactics on Facebook marketing, I've included some resources at http://theleadmachinebook.com/facebook

Personal Profiles vs. Business Pages

On Facebook you have a profile while your business has a page. Both have advantages and disadvantages.

For people who don't like sharing personal information on Facebook, like what they had for lunch or what award their kid just won (I'm so proud of little Johnny graduating first grade!), you don't *need* to have a profile, or make it very public if you prefer to just observe.

However, if you're willing to put yourself out there as a person, it can really help your business. As an entrepreneur, I don't have to worry (as much) about Facebook's algorithms to reach my friends and followers. (Depending on your Facebook set-up, people can follow you without you having to follow them back.)

So, one day I may be talking about the new Spider-Man movie, and the next, promoting the newest episode of the Agents of Change podcast. If the Agents of Change page were to promote the same podcast, even though they have more fans than I have friends, I, as "Rich Brooks," am going to reach more people.

Again, if you're not comfortable putting yourself out there like that, you don't have to. But if you're willing to share some personal nuggets, it can help your business, too.

In short, you're more likely to reach people through your personal account than your business page when you're posting something. However, if all you do is promote your business on your page, you may find that people are tuning you out, muting you, or outright unfriending you.

Find the right balance that makes sense for you.

Ninja trick: Facebook looks at how people are interacting with a post to determine whether they should show it to more people. If the early reports are that people are liking, commenting on, and sharing your post, then Facebook will feel that it is good content and show it to more people. If no one is engaging with a post, Facebook will show it to less people.

Likes are good, but comments are better and shares tend to be the best.

Now, don't tell anyone I told you this, but sometimes before you're going to announce something business-related, you might want to create a personal post that's likely to get a lot of responses, especially comments.

One of my favorite tactics is to ask people to help me with a song list. "I'm putting together a song list about rain. I've got Eddie Rabbit's 'I Love a Rainy Night' and 'Looks Like Rain' by the Dead. What's your favorite rain-soaked song?"

What's great about this question is that there's no one answer. If you were to ask, "Who was the first president of the US?" someone would respond George Washington and basically that would be the end of the discussion.

Now, in my defense, I love music and often create Spotify song lists out of people's suggestions, sharing them back with the people who commented. But I also realize that when I post my next thing, Facebook will likely be thinking, "Rich's last post got a lot of traction...let's spread this one around, too."

Driving Traffic with Posts

Whether you're posting from your profile or your page, you can use your updates to drive traffic to your website or squeeze page.

Now some people believe that people don't want to leave Facebook, so you shouldn't try. I'm not one of those people. Yes, people enjoy Facebook, but if there's a compelling reason to leave, they will.

Different Types of Posts

There are a number of different types of posts in Facebook. Here are a few that will help engage your audience and drive traffic to your site.

Link Posts: When you type a URL into a post on Facebook, Facebook will automatically try pulling a snippet of the page. In a best case scenario, it will be an engaging photo, the title of the page, and an excerpt of text.

If you are sharing something from your own website, you can control what gets shown through certain plugins like Yoast SEO and Facebook's Open Graph.

Besides the excerpt, you can include your own message to encourage people to click through.

Pro Tip: After you type in your URL, you can then delete it. The preview will remain, and your post will look clean and professional.

Photo Posts: Photos are great for engagement. They help your posts stand out and will get people to "slow their scroll."

You can post pictures of something you're working on, a new dish, the view from your office, or a satisfied customer. Inspirational quotes are also powerful, too. Just take a photo (that you have the rights to) and use image editing software to add the quote over the image.

Although I personally feel quotes have been overused, there's no denying that they can be an easy way to create engaging content.

While you can post a link in a photo post, I wouldn't recommend it. Facebook has been cracking down on this tactic because too many publishers were tricking people into clicking on links with photos that had little to nothing to do with the actual post.

Video Posts: With Facebook putting a lot of emphasis on videos right now, it makes sense to at least make some of your posts in this format. You can "go live" or post videos you've previously created and edited.

Facebook tends to promote videos that have been uploaded directly rather than embedded from YouTube or Vimeo. So, if you've got a video that you've put up to YouTube, you may want to directly post it to Facebook rather than embedding it from YouTube. Alternatively, if you want to get a lot of YouTube views, you could embed it on Facebook when you first post it to YouTube, then post another version of it directly to Facebook a week or so later.

Text Posts: If you don't have a link, photo, or video, you're posting a text post. While some marketers feel that these are the least engaging posts, it really depends on what type of content you're sharing.

Humor tends to get a lot of likes and questions tend to get a lot of engagement, as long as you're asking a question that doesn't have one right answer. Remember the George Washington example.

What Type of Post Should You Use?

If you're using Facebook for lead generation, then you'll want to focus your energy around driving traffic to an opt-in page. That means link posts.

However, if all your posts are link posts, then you'll probably suffer from lower engagement, which will lead to less people seeing your content, which will lead to less traffic and leads overall.

Like any healthy meal plan, variety is key. Try different types of posts, and then look at your page's Insights to see which type of posts are getting the most engagement. (Currently you can view your Insights once you've logged into Facebook's Business Manager.)

If you're using your personal profile, you won't get the robust reports that you do with a business page, but you'll still get the feedback that comes with any individual posts, such as likes, comments, and shares.

Using Contests on Facebook

Running contests on Facebook can also generate engagement and drive traffic. In fact, you can also require emails as part of the entry, which builds your email list. The rules of Facebook contests tend to change, but if you use a 3rd party tool like Page-Modo, Heyo, or ShortStack, they'll help you stay in compliance.

Generating Leads Through Events

You can also create events in Facebook. These could be promoting a real-world event, like an 80's Dance Party or a Kids' Coat

Drive, or it could be an online event like a webinar or virtual summit.

What's great about Facebook events is that you can invite your Facebook friends, as well as people who are in a Group with you. Your event will continue to show up in their Events tab and in their notifications unless they specifically say they're not interested. Any changes you make to the event gets promoted to your invitees.

Also, *their* friends may learn about your event because Facebook will often alert people to events their friends are interested in or planning on attending.

As long as you've got a way to capture registration information, you've got a way to generate leads through your events.

If you're running a paid event, or you need to collect registration information, it's important to let people know that just because they said they're attending, that doesn't mean they are registered.

As you can imagine, using events to generate leads can be abused. Don't invite people to events they wouldn't attend (a grand opening of your dry cleaners in Portland, Oregon to an audience that lives in New York City, for instance). Don't continually tweak your event just to show up in people's notifications. Don't invite people to an event more than once a month.

Final Thoughts on Facebook

For most small businesses, Facebook feels like a necessity these days. This is especially true in B2C, but is almost as universally true in B2B. For most of us, the vast majority of our clients are on Facebook, whether they happen to want to hear from us or not.

However, when it comes to strictly organic activity—not including ads or boosted posts—Facebook is a challenge. Unlike

Google, people aren't going to Facebook because they're looking to buy a widget or find a new garden hose...they're going to catch up with friends and family.

Unlike Google, you're not just competing with similar companies, you're competing with every business that wants to get in front of your audience, plus all their friends and family. You're competing for their attention against Aunt Margaret!

Facebook is a good way to establish credibility, show the "human" side of your business, and show potential job applicants what the environment is like at your company. However, for generating leads and making sales, I personally feel there are more important tools out there.

Twitter

Compared to Facebook, Twitter has always felt a little more niche as a social network. Currently it has 310 million users... nothing to sneeze at, but only a fraction of Facebook's user base.

From my own personal experience (and that of similar marketers), it feels like Twitter followers aren't as engaged as Facebook friends. If I post the same message on both platforms, despite the fact my number of Twitter followers dwarfs that of my Facebook friends and followers, my engagement on Facebook (as measured in likes, comments, and shares) routinely crushes my Twitter engagement (as measured in likes, replies, and retweets).

YMMV.

Still, if you *don't* compare Twitter to Facebook, and treat it as its own platform with its own strengths and weaknesses, you will discover ways to attract, engage, and convert people.

Twitter Basics

Since Twitter isn't as ubiquitous as Facebook, let's just get some basics down.

Your Profile

There's no separation between people and businesses on Twitter as there is on Facebook. However, people tend to follow other people more than brands, so keep that in mind.

Regardless of whether you are going on as a person or a brand, you'll need a Twitter handle. Twitter handles must be unique and have up to 15 characters. You'll also have a name of up to 20 characters which doesn't need to be unique.

In other words, there are plenty of Rich Brookses on Twitter, but only one @therichbrooks. (Handles are preceded by the @ symbol.)

You'll need a profile picture (square) and a header image 1,500 x 500 pixels. Assuming you're using Twitter for business, consider the image you're using in both these places. For your personal account, I recommend using your headshot...for your company you could use a logo, a mascot, or a well-known person within the company.

You'll want a short bio of up to 160 characters. Consider this to be a short ad explaining why people should follow you. Your bio can include handles, links, or hashtags. We'll get to those shortly.

You can put in a location. I strongly recommend putting in a relevant location, especially if you're focused on local business.

Lastly, you can include a link. This could be to your home page, blog, or opt-in page, depending on where you want to send them.

Tweets

A tweet is a status update of up to 140 characters. Twitter has been changing lately, and it looks like photos and images won't count towards your character limit.

Likes

Similar to Facebook, you can like a tweet to show you, um, like it, or just to show acknowledgment.

Retweets

Retweeting someone else's tweet is a way of sharing it with your followers. In today's Twitter you can retweet it with or without additional comment.

Mentions

To get someone's attention, or to call them out by name, use their handle, including the @ sign. If you start your tweet with their handle, only people who follow *both* you and that person will see it in their feed. If you include their handle elsewhere in your tweet, then anyone who follows you will see it.

If you want to publicly promote something, like that person being on your podcast, include their handle but don't lead with it. If you don't mind if people see your tweet but aren't trying to promote it to heavily, like wishing them a happy birthday, lead with it.

Hashtags

Hashtags are found throughout social media, but they got their start on Twitter. They were initially used to organize tweets around a certain topic so that people could find others talking about the subject. For example, #oscars, #potus, or #redsox.

On Twitter, if you click on a hashtag (which is automatically converted to a link), it's as if you did a search on that hashtag, pulling up all relevant tweets.

Lists

One of the most underutilized tools of Twitter are lists. Lists are human-curated lists of Twitter accounts. You can create your own lists or subscribe to someone else's public list.

The reason I like lists so much is that they help me make sense of the Twitter feed. They separate the noise from the signal. They let me focus on the people I'm most interested in.

I have a list called Mainers where I pull in everyone I can find from my home state, and most businesses, too. That allows me to keep on top of what's happening locally.

I have another list called Influencers, which are the people in my industry who continually provide the best value and share the best content.

You might also have a list made up of local businesses, or journalists who report on your industry, or your favorite comedians.

If you're using a 3rd party tool like Hootsuite or TweetDeck (my personal favorite), you can create columns based on these lists so you can always see the best, most valuable content, and pay attention to the people who matter to your business.

There's a lot more to Twitter, but this information should get you up and running.

How to Build a Following on Twitter

Many people automatically follow anyone who follows them on Twitter, so one simple way of increasing your following is by following the right people. Twitter does impose limits on how many people you can follow.

You can follow up to 2,000 people, but after that you can only have 10% more people you're following than who are following you.

One way to jumpstart your network on Twitter is to upload your email list. Twitter will take a look at your list and find anyone with a matching email on Twitter. You can then decide to follow everyone Twitter finds or go through the list and pick and choose.

People who already know you in real life are more likely to follow you back, so this is a good place to start.

You can also build a following by promoting your Twitter handle on other platforms, in email, and on your website.

On Twitter, you can mention and network with just about anyone who has a public account, which is most Twitter users. That means you can talk to Shaquille O'Neal, William Shatner, or

Katie Couric. (No promises that they're the ones actually tweeting or looking at their feed, but still.)

And by engaging with people, you're more likely to get someone to follow you.

The Power of Search

When I'm looking to find appropriate people on Twitter, I turn to the advanced search. In advanced search you can of course search for words and hashtags, but you can also filter your search by people, places, or dates.

Imagine you run a yarn store. Go on, imagine it! You can use the advanced search to find people tweeting about "yarn" OR "knitting" OR "poncho kits" within 15 miles of your store. Twitter will show you all the recent tweets, as well as people whose tweets and bios match up with your interest.

You can then follow those people, put them in a list, and otherwise engage with them. They may not know about your store, and might want to check it out.

Driving Traffic and Generating Leads

Like Facebook, Twitter has its own advertising platform. For those not ready to drop money on Twitter, you can still drive traffic to your website and generate leads.

Twitter tends to be a great place to share links, so you can definitely share links to blog posts, podcast episodes, articles, and opt-in pages.

By adding an image to your post you can also capture more real estate in the Twitter feed, often leading to more engagement.

On your own blog and website, make sure you set up Twitter as one of your social sharing buttons, so other people can spread the love on Twitter for you.

Frequently Asked Questions

How often should I tweet?

There's no magic number when it comes to Twitter. Although Twitter will show you tweets from "While You Were Away," it's not as robust as Facebook's algorithm to show you what the most popular, valuable tweets are. In other words, most people who see your tweets see them because they are on Twitter at that moment or because you mentioned them.

Because of that, it's OK to tweet several times a day, sometimes reiterating (but not exactly repeating) previous tweets. After I post a blog, I often tweet out three or four promotional tweets with a link to the post on the first day.

Should I have a personal account or a business account?

Since Twitter treats them the same, it's up to you. If you can manage both, then do both! Because of tools like Hootsuite and TweetDeck, it's easy to run multiple accounts from one screen.

If you want to use Twitter for personal reasons and you don't think your tweets are "on message" with your brand, that's a strong argument to have a separate, personal account.

Should I unfollow someone if they don't follow me back?

You should base whether you follow someone (or not) on whether they provide value to you. That value could be information, inspiration, or education. Or just laughs.

While there are some people who aggressively follow and unfollow people to maximize their numbers, I don't feel it's worth the effort.

Should I automate my tweets?

I'm not a fan of automating tweets, however, I do feel there's a place for scheduling tweets ahead of time. While I don't do this for @therichbrooks, we do pre-schedule multiple tweets per day on our @flytenewmedia and @agentsofchange accounts.

I also try and engage from these accounts as well, responding to anyone who mentions us in a tweet, or sometimes just jumping into a conversation as that account if it seems appropriate.

Should I advertise on Twitter?

If your audience is on Twitter, you should consider advertising. We'll talk more about the ins and outs of Twitter ads in the Digital Advertising section.

LinkedIn

With over 433 million users and growing, LinkedIn is a powerful social network for marketers and business people.

It often doesn't get the love and attention that Facebook, Twitter, or some of the other social media platforms get because it's a little more reserved, a little more professional. However, if you understand the platform, it's a great place to network, to drive traffic to your website, and generate leads.

Start with Your Profile

As with Twitter, you want to start with an engaging profile. That includes:

- **Profile picture.** This should be a professional-looking headshot and not a cropped picture from a party with a disembodied arm around your shoulder.
- **Professional headline.** While your job title might be "President," you should consider using descriptive words that get attention and fit what people are searching for. That's why I describe myself as "Digital Marketing & Social Media Consultant."
- **The other fields.** Complete as many appropriate fields as you can, using keywords (keep in mind people often search on LinkedIn) throughout your current and previous jobs as well as any other fields.
- **Summary.** This is where you want to describe what you do in terms of the needs of your ideal clients.
- **Experience.** Include any relevant jobs or positions, again working in your keywords. More work experience means

more opportunities to network on LinkedIn, as LinkedIn limits your ability to network with people you don't know. If you both worked at IBM or a local clothing shop, even if you didn't work there at the same time, you might be able to connect through LinkedIn.

There's more you can do here, including embedding slide decks from SlideShare, uploading your portfolio, and more. As with any free social media platform, the more "lived in" your profile looks, the more trustworthy you look.

How to Generate Leads at LinkedIn

Generating leads at LinkedIn is about making connections, building trust, and then either driving traffic or making a deeper connection.

Not a love connection, per se, but moving the conversation out of LinkedIn to email, phone, or GoToMeeting.

Building Your LinkedIn Network

As you did with Twitter, you can upload your email database to LinkedIn to see which of your current contacts are already on LinkedIn. Be careful here, because LinkedIn's default is to invite *all* of those people to join you on LinkedIn, even if they're not on LinkedIn already.

It's not your job to get someone on LinkedIn, it's LinkedIn's! Instead, I recommend deselecting all and then manually going through the people who are already on LinkedIn and only connecting with those you want to stay in touch with. These could be customers, prospects, vendors, associates, journalists, local business connections, and so on.

After that initial rush of new connections, I recommend taking it slower, and just adding people as it makes sense. I often will look for someone on LinkedIn if I have an upcoming meeting (or just had one) with them as a way of making a connection.

Also, LinkedIn will often suggest new connections to you...if they make sense, go ahead and connect! However, this isn't a numbers game, so don't worry about trying to add everyone all at once.

While LinkedIn will often send an invitation on your behalf and *not* give you an opportunity to personalize it, (usually on a "People You May Know" page,) if you do get the opportunity to write a personal note, you should. Explain why you're making the connection, and why they may want to connect with you.

The LinkedIn Newsfeed

The LinkedIn newsfeed works like other feeds, where you can update your status, post a picture or video, and engage with other posts.

It's a great place to increase your visibility, both by posting new content as well as by commenting and engaging with others' content. When you comment on someone else's post, LinkedIn alerts them. It's a great way to get on an influencer's radar.

The great thing about LinkedIn is that it doesn't take a lot of time to stay connected. If you spend five minutes a day there, people will think you're the King or Queen of LinkedIn.

LinkedIn Posts

LinkedIn allows you to publish posts, which are like blog posts, except they live on LinkedIn.

Why would you want to publish to LinkedIn rather than your own blog? Well, if you're just starting out, you may not have much of an audience at your own blog, but you can leverage

LinkedIn's audience through their Pulse platform by creating a post.

LinkedIn also allows you to add images, videos, and more to your post, as well as linking back to your website or opt-in page.

Prospecting on LinkedIn

One of my favorite things on LinkedIn is prospecting for new clients for flyte or attendees for our annual conference.

Using the Advanced link next to the search bar at the top of LinkedIn, you can search on job titles, keywords, location, company, and more.

For the Agents of Change, I wanted to connect with social media professionals in New England. Using the keyword "social media," choosing the predetermined New England locations, and filtering out anyone I was already connected to, I got just the results I was looking for.

I was able to save that search for future use. I even set up emails for LinkedIn to alert me when new people match my parameters.

I purposefully didn't just click on the Connect button (which sends a generic invitation), but rather clicked on their profile link, which allows me to send a personalized message, explaining why I want to connect with them.

> *Howdy, Marissa!*
>
> *I saw that we're both doing social media marketing here in Maine, so I thought it would be a good idea for us to connect.*
>
> *Rich*

Now, LinkedIn has a slightly bipolar approach to connections. While the terms of service state that you are only allowed to connect with people you know, LinkedIn is constantly showing you "people you may know" in a way that encourages you to connect regardless of whether you know the person at all.

It's kind of like yelling at a person to diet while shoving a milkshake in their face!

When you send an invite, the recipient has the option of telling LinkedIn that they don't know you. That counts against you, but whether it's a hard number or a percentage, LinkedIn doesn't appear to be saying.

To limit your "I Don't Know" responses, here are a few tips:

- Personalize your invitations.
- Look at the person's profile to see LinkedIn Groups they belong to. You can message fellow Group members, so this may be a way to break the ice so they won't hit the dreaded "I Don't Know" button. (If you don't share any groups, find an appropriate group they belong to and join.)
- Visit the person's website (or company website) to find a way to connect with them.
- If all else fails, use the InMail feature from LinkedIn. However, this costs about $10 an invitation, so use it sparingly.

Once you've made this initial connection on LinkedIn, you can grow it through Messenger.

Messenger

Messenger is basically email within LinkedIn. You can send an email to anyone you're connected to on the platform, even if you don't know their real email. You can also email fellow group members you're not connected to.

The default setting of LinkedIn is to send any messages in Messenger to the recipient's regular email, so it's a great way of getting their attention.

Like any invasive, interrupting tool, be careful how you use it. If you send too many emails to unsuspecting recipients, send spammy emails, or send an email addressed to fifty people, be prepared to have your hand slapped or your account frozen.

However, for creating meaningful, one-on-one engagement, Messenger is hard to beat. You can also use Messenger to drive traffic, or encourage a phone call or in-person meeting.

Groups

Groups used to be one of my favorite places on LinkedIn, where like-minded people could connect and share ideas, stories, and resources. Unfortunately, it became a place where people just promote their own content without engaging with anyone else's.

If you can imagine a room full of people with bullhorns and ear-muffs, you can imagine what most LinkedIn Groups have become.

That's not to say there aren't well run groups where civility and discourse rule the day...just that they've become the exception to the rule.

Unfortunately, the only benefit I see of most groups is a way to connect to people on LinkedIn without running afoul of the rules.

Company Pages

I'm not sure why LinkedIn hasn't done more with Company Pages, seeing how successful Facebook has been with Business Pages, but they haven't.

If you're a larger company and you're constantly recruiting, having a page is important. I would probably make the argument that if you're a publicly-traded company, then having a company page offers some benefit as well.

However, for most small businesses, a Company Page is simply a matter of "set it and forget it."

SnapChat, Instagram, and Pinterest, Oh My!

There are so many other social media platforms and networks, and more coming online all the time.

Some stick around, like Instagram and Pinterest, and others fall away, like Ello and Google+. It's hard to know which will succeed and which will fail, so rather than giving you a lot of reading on platforms that may not impact you or be around in the future, let me just give you some guidelines on how to assess new platforms, or platforms you haven't explored yet.

Does my ideal customer use this platform?

Because if they don't, there's little point in investing your time and energy here when it can be better spent elsewhere.

Can I engage with my ideal customer on this platform?

Even if your ideal customer is here, you may have no easy way to engage with them. While every platform is different, providing value is the best way to attract attention and engage with your customer.

How do I convert my ideal customer on this platform?

Each platform has its own strengths and weaknesses when it comes to lead generation. For instance, it's relatively easy to get followers on Instagram, but the only place you can include a clickable link to your website is on your bio. That makes driving traffic from Instagram a challenge, unless you're using their advertising platform.

On SnapChat, you'll have to give people verbal and visual cues, as well as a strong incentive, to get them off SnapChat and to an opt-in page.

Digital Advertising

When I was young(er) and naive(er), I couldn't understand why people were so infatuated with digital advertising, whether it was banner ads, paid search (Google Ads), or paid text links.

"Why pay for leads when you could get them for free?" I thought.

Of course, the leads you get from SEO, blogging, and other platforms are not free. They require time, resources, or hiring an outside company that can optimize your website and write your blog posts for you.

Also, when you first start your business, you'll likely have more time than money. But as time progresses, and you start to build up a customer base, you find that you no longer have the time (or the energy) to constantly be creating content to attract that "free" traffic.

Back when I was focused entirely on organic leads, it was easier to get someone's attention; there was just a lot less content back then. But now you're competing with other companies providing similar services, industry bloggers, niche bloggers, consultant bloggers, news sites, sports sites, weather sites, cat memes, Lord of the Rings memes, Spider-Man memes, and everything else the internet can throw at you.

While developing content to attract your ideal customer is always a great idea, digital ads can provide an excellent source of new leads that you may not have reached otherwise. In fact, competition for your prospects' attention is so fierce in some industries, many people are spending advertising dollars just to get visitors to their free content!

Of course, it helps if the free content is part of a strategy to get someone to opt into your email list or take some other desired action.

Digital advertising is especially important if you're just launching a new website or service. New sites don't tend to rank well organically, so paid search can be the starter fluid you need to get things cooking.

Also, if you're getting into a new line of products, where you don't have a lot of content and aren't known as a trusted resource, well designed ads can drive that necessary traffic.

Although there are plenty of places you can advertise your company or website, we're going to focus on three in this section: Google Adwords, Facebook Ads, and Twitter Ads.

We'll touch upon Instagram ads because it's owned by Facebook and you advertise on Instagram directly through Facebook. I didn't include LinkedIn because my experience, and the experience of others I trust, has led me to believe it's not a good platform for small businesses.

We will talk about retargeting, another form of advertising, but not until the section on Retain.

Google Adwords

In the past, when I talked to clients about Adwords—Google's pay-per-click platform—the general response was, "Those ads on the right hand side? I never click on them. I don't know anyone who clicks on those ads."

However, The Motley Fool reports that Google made 17.3 billion (with a "B") in the *first quarter* of 2015...nearly all of it from paid ads.

So apparently *someone* is clicking on those ads.

Google's recent switch to a single column for search results means that Adwords gets even more visibility and prominence on the search results page.

Before searchers get to organic results, before they get to local results, they'll see paid results, assuming there are relevant paid ads to show.

Adwords allows you to get in front of your prospects when they are actively searching for a solution you can provide. However, since every click—no matter how unqualified—costs you, you need to be very strategic with your Adwords.

Choose the Right Words with Keyword Planner

Google's Keyword Planner, which we first looked at in the SEO section, is a great place to start generating some ideas on what the right keywords are to go after. You can use the five perspectives we discussed and start playing around to determine search volume, competition, and recommended bids, based on other bids.

Focus on High Commercial Intent

A person is more likely to click on an ad when she has "high commercial intent." In other words, if someone is searching for "white house," they are probably doing research, not planning on buying something. If they search on "white house memorial plate," they probably have high commercial intent.

As you review your Keyword Planner results, use the lens of "high commercial intent." Don't spend money on keywords that are tangential to your business. Don't use keywords that are too broad. If you make popcorn poppers, don't bid on "popcorn." There are a thousand reasons why someone might Google popcorn, and finding a commercial grade popcorn popper is probably at the bottom of that list.

Narrow Your Focus Further

If you only serve people in a limited area, or if your best audience is in a specific geographic region, you can limit your ads to show only to people in that area.

If you run a dry cleaners, you can "day part" your ads so they only show when you're open. Or if your audience is more likely to be looking for you during the work day, you can stop your ad on the weekends.

If you want to avoid certain types of searches (or searchers), you can use negative keywords. If you have a vegan restaurant, you might use "recipe" as a negative keyword to prevent your ads from showing if someone's looking to cook at home.

Improve Your Ad Quality and Pay Less

Although Adwords is an auction, it's not just about who's willing to pay the most when it comes to grabbing the top spot.

Remember: advertisers don't pay when their ad is shown, only when someone clicks on their ad. So, if people aren't clicking on ads, Google isn't making any money!

To make sure it's showing ads that people are clicking on, Google has a quality score that can move you up (or down) in terms of your ad. There are a number of factors that go into your score, including:

- The click-through rate (CTR) of your ad
- How relevant your ad copy is
- The quality and relevance of your landing page
- Your past performance in Adwords

By improving the quality score of your ads, you can bring down your ad costs by as much as 50%!

Be Hands-On

Don't turn on your ads and forget about them. You can quickly spend thousands of dollars poorly this way.

Especially at the beginning, you should be actively managing your ads. Check in to see the click through and conversion rates of your different ads. If one's not working, or underperforming, pause it or shut it off completely. Put your budget towards a keyword that's more effective.

Optimize Your Landing Pages

If someone does a search, clicks on your ad, and then arrives at your home page where there are dozens of options for them to choose from, they're more likely than not to just click the back button and choose a different ad.

Not only did you just lose the potential sale, you paid for that visit!

Generally, it's best practice to send people to a squeeze page, or at least a very specific product page that's relevant to the search they just performed.

If the goal of your ad is to generate a lead, your landing page should repeat the ad's offer and have some sort of opt-in.

Should You Work with an Outside Agency?

Google has set up Adwords so that just about anyone can run ads, and many small businesses do just that. One nice thing about managing your Adwords in-house is avoiding management fees that an outside agency will charge you.

Agencies often have minimums, too. It's a common refrain from agencies that you really need to spend $1,500/mo to see any real results in Adwords. That's true, if you've hired an agency. That's because often their fees come out of these monthly charges, and they need to make a profit, too.

However, if you're already up to your eyes in work, and you don't have a lot of experience in Adwords, and you need to see results immediately, hiring an agency can be a good decision. You can even hire most agencies to get things set up for you and get them running.

Well-managed Adwords campaigns tend to perform better over time, as the person managing them can start to weed out underperforming ads, run A/B split tests to find the best ad copy, and focus the budget on ads with good click-through and conversions.

Once this work has been done, you should be able to pick up the campaigns and continue them without an outside resource, assuming you're willing to put the time into managing the ads.

Facebook Ads

With Adwords, you're targeting people when they are actively searching for your solution. With Facebook, chances are your product or service is the last thing on their mind. However, Facebook's powerful targeting (and retargeting) tools make this a powerful platform for any company, especially B2C companies.

Generating leads from Facebook ads can be broken down into three steps: target, advertise, and convert.

Facebook provides two very similar tools for you to target your audience, create your ads, and set your budgets: Ads Manager and Power Editor. Ads Manager is a little more user friendly, especially for the newbie, and Power Editor offers more tools and control. If Power Editor doesn't scare you off, I'd recommend using it.

Ways to Target and Reach Your Ideal Customers

The first thing you're going to want to do is define the audience for your ads. You can accomplish this through three popular methods: creating a custom audience, creating a lookalike audience, or creating an audience with Facebook's demographics.

Here's how to accomplish all three:

Create a Custom Audience

There are several ways to create a custom audience, and once you have created one, you can use this audience for any ads you want to run, now or in the future.

Upload your database.

One cool feature of Facebook ads is the ability to upload your own database of email addresses. What this means is that you can target people who already know you...warm leads, so to speak.

The addresses can be from your customer database or it can be your email subscribers. Of course, it only works if the email addresses you have on file are the same addresses people used to sign up for Facebook. If your list is made up of official business emails, you may not have as many matches.

Target your site visitors.

You can also serve ads up to people who have already visited your website. This is called retargeting (or remarketing), and we'll get into the details in the Retain section. It requires that you put a tracking pixel on specific pages within your site... something your web developer can do if you don't feel comfortable doing it yourself.

Here's an example of how you might use this technique: Let's say you have a river cruise company, and you have a page for your company outing offerings. Someone visits that page, but doesn't click to the reservation page. You could then create a custom audience based on visiting one page but not the other, and serve up ads to this audience reminding them of what a great team-building experience your cruises are.

You can, and should, use Facebook's filtering tools to further control who sees your ads. For example, just because someone's in your database, that doesn't mean they are appropriate for a specific ad. If you run a wine shop and you're having a wine and cheese pairing, you may decide to advertise only to people within ten miles of your store, regardless of whether they've visited your website.

Create a lookalike audience.

I love lookalike audiences. They are a quick way of reaching people who are similar to an audience you have already saved. It's like you are telling Facebook, "Here are people who are interested in my product. Please go out and find more like them."

Facebook then uses its obscene amount of information about its user base to find appropriate matches and create the new audience.

If you've got an opt-in email list of pet owners you upload to Facebook, a lookalike audience will find many more people out there that are like this audience. Just like before, be sure to use Facebook's filtering tools to further narrow this audience, improving the targeting.

Create an audience with Facebook's demographics.

Maybe you don't have a database of emails, or maybe the people who visited your website aren't your target audience. If this is the case, you can still tap into Facebook's demographics.

With 1.5 billion active users, chances are your audience is on Facebook. You can create an audience based on location, age, gender, and languages.

You can fine tune your audience based on demographics, interests, behaviors, and more. Want to target CEOs? No problem. Want to target moms (or dads, for that matter) in the Greater Chicago area who are also small business owners? No problem. Want to target commuters who spend a lot of time on their Android phones? No problem.

Once you've created your audience, whether it's a custom audience, a lookalike audience, or one you've created from Facebook's user base, you'll be able to save and use this audience for future ads as well.

Create Your Ads

There are many goals Facebook ads can help you achieve, including page or post engagement, app downloads, or video views, to name a few. However, if your goal is generating more leads, then you'll want to concentrate on website traffic, website conversions, or lead generation (where the leads are captured right on Facebook).

You can create a new ad or choose an existing post. Some Facebook marketers like to use posts that received good organic engagement as a way of testing out different ad ideas.

If you're creating something new, you can choose from an ad with an image or video, or with multiple images in a carousel. The carousel can be a good choice if you've got a lot of products that you want to show off. A golf store might show drivers, putters, and golf bags in the carousel.

You can also determine where you want your ads to show: in the newsfeed, in the right column, on mobile devices, or on Instagram. Since this is the only way to make your Instagram posts clickable to a webpage or opt-in, this is a very powerful tool.

You'll also want to set your budget. You can control when and for how long your ad will run, how much you're willing to spend per day or over the course of the campaign, as well as some other features.

Optimize Your Landing Pages

Just like your Adwords campaigns, you'll want to have specialty squeeze pages for your Facebook ad campaigns as well. Whether you can reuse or repurpose your squeeze pages or if you have to create unique landing pages is up to you.

Final Takeaways

As of the writing of this book, Facebook ads are one of the most popular, most cost-effective ways to advertise on the web. If you want to get in front of your ideal demographic, Facebook will let you do just that.

While I expect the cost of Facebook ads to continue to go up, especially as Facebook "runs out of space," they continue to be an affordable way to reach your customers and prospects.

However, keep an eye on more than just your cost per click. When someone sees a Google ad, they see it after they search for a product or service. On Facebook, they're usually just catching up with friends when you woo them away.

Our own experience has been that Facebook ads are less expensive, but Google Ads convert at a higher rate, often making them equally cost-effective (or ineffective).

Twitter Ads

Advertising on Twitter is similar to advertising on Facebook, in that people are not actively searching for your product or service when they are on the platform. While Twitter does allow you to target people based on some interesting criteria, its targeting capabilities aren't as powerful (or creepy) as Facebook's.

As an example, Twitter isn't even sure if users are male or female, as it doesn't ask for that information when you sign up. However, it takes an educated guess based on your name and other telltale signs so that it can offer gender-based targeting to its advertisers.

Twitter ads are currently less expensive than either Facebook's or Google's, although my personal experience has been that the ROI isn't as good.

With all that conflicting information about the Twitter ad platform, there's only one question you should be asking yourself: is my audience on Twitter?

If they are, you should experiment with ads on Twitter. And if they're not, you'll be just as successful buying billboards on a highway your customers never drive.

Creating a New Campaign

By logging into Twitter and clicking on your profile pic in the bar at the top of the page, you can navigate to ads.twitter.com. Here, you can create a new campaign.

There are a number of goals Twitter ads can help you accomplish, including getting more followers, getting more people to watch your videos, or getting engagement on your tweets. However, we're going to focus on Website clicks or conversions and Leads on Twitter.

Creating an Audience

Once you have chosen a campaign type, it's time to develop an audience.

Twitter requires that you choose a location to start, but it can be as large as a country or even multiple countries, or as small as a metro area or postal code.

You can filter by gender, language, and mobile information such as carrier or operating system.

Once you decide how narrow or broad an audience you are going for, it's time to get into their interests. One way to get in front of your ideal customers is **targeting them based on the keywords they're using**.

If you're a taco shop, you could target local people who use words like "hungry," "taco," or "Mexican" right around lunch time.

You can add followers to the mix. By targeting a specific user name or names, Twitter will find people similar to the followers of those usernames.

You can target by interests, which include categories like Automotive, Beauty, and Education, each with further subcategories. For example, if you sell shaving products, you can target Twitter users who have shown interest in "shaving and grooming."

And, as with Facebook, you can create a list of warm leads on Twitter called "Tailored Audiences." You can upload an email database, tag people who have visited your website, or collect people who have used your mobile app. You can also expand your audience by "targeting similar users," aka "lookalike audiences."

Because so many people watch TV while on Twitter, you can target people during specific shows. People often watch the #Oscars or #TheWalkingDead and want to share that experience with other people on Twitter. If your audience is aligned around a specific TV show, this could be a great way of getting their attention.

You can target based on user interests as well. God and the NSA only know where they get this information, but you can target people who are likely to dine at Applebee's or like to buy gifts and flowers.

Finally, you can exclude people based on tailored audiences or behaviors. This is helpful if you want to target people for a first-time buyer discount, but don't want to show that discount to people you've already done business with.

Setting Your Budget

You can set a daily budget, a lifetime budget, and choose different campaign optimizations, depending on which campaign goals you chose.

Creating Your Ad

Now that you know who you are trying to reach and how much you're willing to spend to reach them, it's time to create your ad.

If you chose Website clicks and conversions, then you'll want create a new tweet (although you can choose one you've already posted), along with a "card." The card is basically an image that should capture your ideal customer's eye and imagination. Unlike Facebook, that has a 20% text limit, you can use any combination of text and image in your ad.

You're also able to create a headline and include the URL you want to send people to, should they click on your ad.

Optimize Your Landing Pages

Just like with your Adwords and Facebook ad campaigns, you don't want to send people to your home page. Instead, create a custom landing page that matches the offer or ad your prospect just clicked on.

Takeaways

Twitter lacks Facebook's granular targeting tools, and it doesn't reach as wide an audience. However, if your audience is on Twitter, Twitter ads can be a very cost-effective way of reaching them, as the ad rates are often lower than Facebook's or Google's.

If you have the budget and the resources to add another advertising channel to the mix, Twitter is a good place to experiment.

Advertising on Other Social Sites

These days, almost every social site has an advertising platform, and if they don't now, they will soon.

LinkedIn, Pinterest, and Snapchat all allow you to buy ads. For sites that don't yet, it's only because they're trying to build up a big enough audience where advertisers will be attracted but users won't find it easy to leave when they suddenly start seeing ads in their feed.

Whatever platform you look at for advertising, you should use these questions:

Is my audience on the platform?

If your audience isn't here, put down your checkbook. Or PayPal. Or Apple Pay. You wouldn't advertise burgers at a vegan hangout, right?

What are my goals for advertising?

As we saw in some of the other platforms, different campaigns can have different goals, including brand awareness, engagement, and, of course, lead generation. Although it's not the focus of this book, there's nothing wrong with paying for likes or follows.

If my goal is lead generation, what offer can I make?

In general, people don't want to leave a fun, social site where their friends are to visit your website.

You'll need to give them a reason (your offer) that makes it worth their while to abandon their friends and come check you out.

Once there, you'll need a squeeze page to capture their contact information so that you can follow up with them.

What is a lead worth?

Math has never been my strong suit, so determining the value of a lead is always tricky. One way to look at this is to start by determining the lifetime value of a customer (CLV). If you have an architectural firm and the average job is 1.2 million with a gross profit of $400,000, and your average customer hires you for two jobs, your CLV is $800,000.

If you run a sandwich shop and the average sale is $10 with a gross profit of $3, and the average customer comes in once a week for 5 years, then your CLV is $780 (3 x 52 x 5). Lucky for you, there are more people who need sandwiches than commercial buildings.

The CLV is an important variable, but so is your lead to customer conversion rate. If one out of one hundred leads for your architectural firm becomes a customer, then a lead is worth $8,000. If one out of five leads for your sandwich shop becomes a customer, then a lead is worth $156.

Now you know what a lead is worth. (Congrats!) However, not everyone who sees an ad or clicks on it will become a lead. Using these platforms, you can quickly determine how much you're spending to get in front of people and drive them to your website. As long as you're staying below what a lead is worth to your business, you're in good shape.

What am I willing to spend?

For some businesses, like those selling a digital product, the total amount you're willing to spend isn't so important. As long as you're spending less to acquire each customer than the CLV, it's like printing money.

For other businesses, like an attorney or web design firm, where you only have so many hours, you'll need to make sure you don't get more business than you can handle, which amounts to paying for leads you can't use.

Also, chances are you're not going to nail your ads the first time out. Most campaigns get more effective over time, assuming you're actively managing them. You may want to set limits on campaigns early on so that you don't waste your money on underperforming ads.

How will I measure my results?

Most, if not all, platforms offer some sort of metrics on how your campaigns are doing. You should also be measuring the results using traffic reports like Google Analytics.

In some cases, that may still not be enough. Social platforms and Google Analytics can show you how many people filled out your form, but they can't tell you whether these people were good leads or not.

Depending on your business, and your interest in digging a little deeper, you can rate the leads as they come in or after you've made contact with them, to get a real sense of whether the leads from a campaign were above, at, or below the value of other leads you've gotten in the past.

How will I improve my results?

Most campaigns, as I've stated before, get better over time. However, that doesn't happen magically.

You should plan on running at least two ads side by side; the traditional A/B split. These ads should be nearly identical, with one element changed. Maybe it's the headline, or the image, or the offer, with all other elements the same.

If the ad with the "Free Shipping" headline beats the "Summer Sale" headline, then you take the Free Shipping ad and find something else to split test. Maybe one has a photo of the product, the other of a happy customer using it.

Wrapping Up

At this stage we've focused on building a website that's designed for results and conversions. We've also looked at three different ways to attract our ideal customers to this site:

- **Search:** Putting our business in front of people who are actively searching for what we have to offer
- **Social:** Engaging our audience on different platforms and networks, building trust, and nudging them over to our website
- **Ads:** Targeting our ideal customers while they search or socialize and driving them to an offer

However, not everyone is going to buy on the first visit to your website, and most will never return. So in the next section, we'll be looking at how to retain their interest and stay in communication with them.

Retain

Oh baby, give me one more chance
(To show you that I love you)
Ooh ooh baby
(I want you back)
Yeah yeah yeah yeah
(I want you back)
Na na na na

— Jackson 5

(Songwriters: Alphonso Mizell / Berry Gordy
Jr / Deke Richards / Freddie Perren)

You've build a website that converts. You've driven traffic through search, social, or ads. You're all set, right?

Not really.

Many people come to your website looking for information, or they're doing research. They look at your website, then five more. This is true whether you're a lawyer, an innkeeper, or sell a product.

So, how can you stay in front of these people? How can you keep those lines of communication open?

Traditionally, or as traditional as digital marketing gets, it's been about email marketing. Getting someone to opt into your email list so you can stay in communication.

With the introduction of social media, you can get people to like your page, follow you on Twitter, become LinkedIn with you, or subscribe to your YouTube channel, podcast, or blog.

More recently, you are now able to retarget your site visitors: follow them around the web with ads and enticements to come back to your website.

The purpose of all these approaches is to retain their attention and your ability to communicate with them. So in this section, we'll take a closer look at building your email list, retarget them with ads, and close with some tips on how to get people to engage with you on social.

Email Marketing

With all the attention on social media, email marketing seems considerably, well, unsexy.

We've been told that social media is where companies and brands need to be. That "kids" coming out of college don't even use email any more. That email is for "old people."

Do you really need an email list?

I've presented at a number of social media and digital marketing conferences over the years, sitting in the speakers' room with a number of well-known social media experts. (Sorry, I'm not about to name drop...it's not that kind of book!)

Often, there would be some good natured ribbing and bragging that would happen between these gurus, to see who was really a bigger deal. What did they brag about? How many followers they had on Twitter? How many YouTube views they had racked up? How many friends they had on Facebook?

No. They bragged about the size of their email list.

Because all of these social media experts know that the power is in the list. There are few things more valuable to a small business than an opt-in email list.

Why Email is More Powerful than Social Media

Although we're going to look at how to get people to follow you on social media and how to run retargeting campaigns, it's my opinion that the most valuable way to retain a connection with your prospects—and to generate more business from your customers—is with email.

Social media is great for warming leads...

But email marketing is great for closing deals. As we've discussed, it can be difficult to sell in social media. People are often there just to connect and catch up with friends. However, once you've gotten someone to opt into your email mailing list, they've given you permission to market and sell to them.

Right in their inbox.

Email sticks around

During the time it takes you to read this chapter, you might be missing hundreds or thousands of tweets, snaps, and status updates, which are never to be seen again. However, every email will still be in your inbox, awaiting your return and attention.

Even if you don't open and engage with that email...even if you send it directly to the trash, you're still going to see it. See who sent it, see the subject line and possibly a bit of the email itself.

Email is a lot less fleeting than social media.

You own your email list

Businesses and entrepreneurs have put time, energy, and money into building a following on platforms like Facebook, LinkedIn, and Twitter. But the truth is, at any point these platforms could go out of business, or just become irrelevant.

Businesses sunk plenty of resources into Facebook, only to have the algorithm change so that they could no longer reach their own fans! Other platforms are likely to follow suit.

When you build on a social media platform, it's like building a house on someone else's property. You're at their mercy. They can change the rules, change their algorithm, start charging rent, or simply go out of business, and you have no recourse.

I'm not saying don't use these platforms, just be aware of their shortcomings.

On the other hand, you *own* your email list. Even when you're using a service provider like Constant Contact or MailChimp, you own your list. You can take it at any point and move it to another provider. You can download it and use it for other marketing. You can add it to your business database. You can upload it to a social networking site to jumpstart your networking or to target warm leads.

You can even print it up on 3 x 5 cards and roll around in it for fun. (I was going to say "naked" but I don't want you to get paper cuts.)

Email marketing is affordable, easy to do, and incredibly effective when done well.

Every year I talk to hundreds of businesses and entrepreneurs about generating more leads online, and in almost every situation I recommend building an email list...and starting on that list yesterday.

In the next few chapters, we'll take a look at how to build your email list, even if you're starting from scratch. How to send out emails, and how to get them delivered, opened, read, and acted upon.

Because although you never get a second chance to make a first impression, if you get someone to join your list, you get a second (and third, and fourth, etc.,) chance to make a sale.

Getting Started with Email Marketing

If you're just getting started with email marketing, one thing you're going to need is an email service provider (ESP).

Now, that's different from your Internet Service Provider (ISP), the company that may be giving you an email address, or at least the ability to send and receive emails.

If you're going to be sending out mass (opt-in) emails, you can't be doing that through Gmail or Outlook. Spam is all too common these days, so ISPs, hosting companies, and similar organizations are cracking down on any type of bulk email. If you send out too many bulk emails or get too many bounces or too many spam reports, they may shut down your ability to send any emails or even shut down your website!

To avoid this, you'll want to use an ESP like Constant Contact, MailChimp, or AWeber. (You could also use a CRM like Ontraport, Infusionsoft, or Salesforce, that has bulk email capabilities.)

Now, "bulk email" has a negative connotation, so let me just be clear that I'm only recommending that you send valuable emails to an audience that has opted in to hear from you.

The Benefits of an ESP

Some small business people don't like the idea that ESPs charge money based on the number of emails you send out or the size of your list. However, this is just the cost of doing business.

Here are just a few of the reasons why an ESP is some of the best money you can spend on digital marketing:

ESPs keep you on the right side of the law. Most countries have rules around unsolicited emails. Almost all require an unsubscribe link in each email that goes out, allowing people to stop receiving emails from you immediately.

If someone clicks on that link, your ESP will stop sending them emails on your behalf, which is actually a good thing! You don't want to get labeled as a spammer, and you only want to be sending emails to people who want to hear from you.

ESPs automatically add other required information, such as a street address in every email.

Ability to schedule email delivery. You can have emails go out at a specific time, even if you're not at your computer. If you know that your audience is likely at their inbox at 2pm, you can schedule your email blast for then.

Ability to send out responsive emails. The number one activity on smartphones is checking emails. If you're sending out emails that don't read well on a smartphone, your subscribers will delete them without even reading them.

Ability to set up autoresponders. You can also have a series of emails go out to your audience, say one a day for a week, after they've signed up. You can turn this into a free mini-course to help build trust and attract new subscribers.

Ability to customize your emails to your recipient. Speaking of subscribers, people are often more responsive when they see their name at the beginning of an email or even in the subject line. (Which is odd, because we never include someone's name in the subject line if we're just writing to them as one human being to another.)

Depending on what information you've collected from your subscribers, you can greet them by name, mention their home town, or even pull in a paragraph based on their interests.

Ability to segment your lists. Since every email includes an invitation to unsubscribe, it's important to send emails only to people who might be interested. ESPs allow you to set up segments within your list. A pet store may have different content based on whether someone owns a dog, cat, or falcon.

You can create segments within your list when people are first signing up by asking what their interests are; this will automatically add them to specific lists. Also, you can create or assign segments based on what links people click on.

If you send out pet store emails with links about dogs, cats, and falcons, people can be added to each segment based on what they click on.

Ability to send A/B split tests. Are people going to respond better to "20% off" or "free shipping"? One way to find out is to send out otherwise identical emails to your subscribers, where they'll get one or the other randomly, and see which one gets the bigger open and click through rate.

Ability to measure your results. ESPs provide fantastic reporting tools. You'll know how many people are on your list. How many opened each email. How many people clicked on each link. How many people unsubscribed from each email, and more.

Combining your ESPs reports with Google Analytics will give you incredible insights into how your email marketing campaigns are working, and how you can improve on the results.

Taken all together, the ability to send out emails and get in front of people who are interested in what you have to say or sell, to avoid the pitfalls of non-compliance, for just pennies per delivery, is a great investment.

Building Your Email List

As we've discussed, email marketing is an incredibly powerful tool. However, there's also a lot of competition for the inbox. Some are legitimate email marketers like you, who are only emailing to a list of opt-in subscribers. Others are aggressive, black hat marketers who add everyone to a list. Still others wear a gray hat, treating their prospect and customer database as an opt-in email list.

Regardless, people have email fatigue. They're not just going to sign up for your email list if your come-on is "Join our Email List." That's code for, "Please Let Us Spam You into Submission."

They're giving you something of value: access to their inbox.

Your customers' inbox is the most valuable piece of real estate on the Internet.

And to get that level of access, you need to provide them something of overwhelming value. Something that they will be willing to trade a small part of their privacy for. Something that is referred to as a lead magnet.

Different businesses might use different offers as lead magnets. A toy store might offer 10% off coupons to people who sign up. A leadership consultant might offer an eBook on *How to Lead a Team of Millennials*. A software company might offer a free or extended trial.

The important thing is to create a lead magnet that is attractive to your ideal customer and no one else. Giving away a free HDTV with every signup is a great way to build your list, and drive yourself out of business under the weight of unqualified leads.

The System for Email Registrations

Whatever lead magnet you decide on, here's a short version of how you're going to create the process to generate as many sign-ups as possible:

- **Sign up with an ESP.** Whoever you choose, they'll provide you a snippet of code that you can use to create a signup box on your website.

- **Customize the signup box.** Don't stick with Join Our Mailing List. Tell visitors why they should subscribe. Tell them about the lead magnet. Put it on every page. Try different approaches.

- **Create a Thank You page.** Although many ESPs provide you with their own Thank You page, you should instead create one on your website to send people to after they sign up. The benefits are branding and the ability to let people know to keep their eye open for a confirmation and welcome email from you. (Bonus: you can also try upselling them at this point. After all, they've already shown that they're interested in what you have to sell, you might as well strike while the iron is hot.)

- **Customize the confirmation message.** If you are requiring double opt-in—where your subscriber has to click on a link in their email to confirm that they want to be on your list—then you'll need to send a confirmation message. Don't worry, this is something your ESP will provide. However, it's a good idea to tweak the language so that it sounds like it's coming from you. But don't make it so customized that you get away from the critical piece of information: they need to click on the link to get access to your lead magnet. If you confuse them, they may not realize they have to click and you'll lose them forever.

- **Customize the welcome message.** If you have a double opt-in, your subscribers receive this message after confirmation. If you had a single opt-in (they just have to subscribe at your website), they receive this message after they sign up. In the welcome message you can be as creative and clever as you like. Also, *here* is where you include the link to your lead magnet (or the discount code for your store), as we now know we have the prospect's legitimate email address.

What to Do after You've Signed Someone Up

What you *don't* want to do after you've captured someone's attention is have a long, dry spell before reaching out to them again. First off, their interest may have cooled. Second, they may have forgotten who you are or what they signed up for.

Besides the welcome message, you should consider an autoresponder campaign where you offer them some added benefit or value, even if it's just a one-email campaign. Or maybe the autoresponder is five emails that link to your most popular blog posts, delivered once a day or once every other day. Or maybe it's a second coupon that's only good for seven days, encouraging them to get into the mindset that they are your customer.

Whatever the case is, take advantage of that moment of interest.

Different Ways to Capture Emails

By now you know that you want to move past the Join Our Mailing List come-on. But what are some of the methods you could use to capture attention and emails while someone's at your website?

Here are a just few:

- A signup box with the lead magnet in the secondary column of all your pages

- A big header bar across your home page featuring the lead magnet
- An inline text link that asks people to join your list
- A call to action on your blog that tells people to sign up for free updates
- A modal window / light box / popup window that shows up after 15 or 30 seconds with your call to action
- A "sticky" header or footer that's always there (until someone clicks the "x" to close it) promoting your email newsletter
- Customized lead magnets based on the page or blog post that someone is reading

Which method will work best? There's no way to know until you've tried them. I was sure that a modal window promoting a free download on our Agents of Change website would work better than the footer that just promoted "Get the latest AOC updates!" And I was dead wrong. The footer turned out to be significantly more successful.

That's why we test things, people!

Now, it may be that people saw the modal window (which is just a fancy popup window where everything around it goes gray and you have to click to close it), but they weren't ready to commit. A few pages (or visits) later, they were hooked, and the footer bar made it easy for them to sign up. So, those two working in concert could be the best solution for that website. You'll need to do your own testing to find out what works best for you.

Using Tools Beyond an ESP

Not all ESPs have all these fancy ways of getting people to sign up. Modal windows, sticky headers and footers, etc., don't always come standard.

For our own sites, and many of our clients' sites, we use Lead-Pages. This is a SAAS (software as a service) company that provides a number of different tools for email signups. Besides modal windows that are activated after a specific period of time, number of page views, or activities, one of my favorite features of LeadPages is the ability to customize a lead magnet for each page.

Say you run a home improvement business. You've got pages on bathroom remodeling, kitchen remodeling, and turning your backyard into an outdoor room. With LeadPages, you can customize your lead magnet so that the people interested in bathroom remodeling might be offered a download of the best new shower ideas, kitchen remodelers might see an offer about how to improve your home's value through remodeling, and the backyard enthusiasts might see 10 Outdoor Grills to Make Your Backyard the Envy of the Neighborhood.

The more you can customize that lead magnet, the more sign-ups you will get.

Put Your Email List into Action

It's one thing to build your list, it's another to profit from it.

In this book, I'm treating an email signup like a lead. However, there's more you can do to warm up this lead and turn it into a sale. In fact, there are four distinct things you need to do to make the most of your emails: get them delivered, opened, read, and acted upon.

How to Get Your Emails Delivered

If you're using an ESP and your list is all opt-in, you're well on your way to getting your emails delivered. However, there are at least three places your emails can be stopped.

Your recipient's ISP. The ISP of your subscriber doesn't want to be in the business of delivering spam. To that end, it's set up some of its own protocols to stop emails from arriving in its customer's inboxes. Subject lines, body copy, emails to bcc'd addresses, and emails from disreputable addresses or domains can all stop you dead in your tracks.

Your recipient's company. Assuming your subscriber works for a company, the company's IT staff may be looking to corral emails that could be irrelevant or even dangerous, such as one carrying malware. Even if it makes it through the internet to the person's business, it may not make it any further.

Your recipient's junk filter. We've all found important emails in our junk or spam folder. For whatever reason, it trips a switch, causing the email program to tag it as junk and hide it away in a dusty folder people only check when absolutely necessary, rubbing elbows with deposed Nigerian princes, Russian brides, and Canadian pharmacies.

To avoid these many traps, it helps to follow some best practices.

- Don't use all caps in your subject line
- Avoid spammer words like "free," "$$$," or "meet singles."
- Don't use a lot of exclamation points, special characters, or emojis.

These rules are constantly changing, but the good news is that most ESPs can run your emails through a spam checker to see if you're likely to get blocked.

How to Get Your Emails Opened

Even when emails end up in your recipient's inbox, it doesn't mean that they get opened. Many of us, especially when we're on our phone, just take one look at the subject line and who the email is from and start throwing things in the trash.

To get someone to open your email, you need to convince them it's worth their time. This can be tricky, because if you get too sensational, one of those pesky junk filters will swoop out of nowhere and keep your email from ever arriving.

There are a number of tactics you can use to get people to open your emails. Here are a few of my favorites:

- **Intrigue.** Often referred to as the "information gap" or the "curiosity gap." You tease some information in your subject line, but keep the rest hidden. People get curious, their mind looking to bridge the gap, so they open your email. Example: "The one thing I wish I did to prepare my kid for kindergarten."
- **Familiarity.** Making your marketing emails sound like a personal email. This prevents people from putting up

their shields. Example: "Will I see you tomorrow?" (Perfect for tomorrow's webinar.)

- **Personalization.** Adding their name (or other custom information) to an email. This is often done in the body copy, but it can be used in the header, too. Example: "[Name], I'd like to introduce you to Larry."
- **Timing.** While your emails have longer shelf-lives than tweets or status updates, you can still use timing to get people to open your email. Example: "What are you making for dinner?" (Good if you are selling ready-made meals.)
- **Scarcity.** A time honored tactic among marketers. Creating real or perceived scarcity can spur subscribers into action. Example: "Only 48 hours until the early bird discounts are gone!"

Here's what doesn't work:

- Dr. Johnson's Monthly Article
- Quarterly Newsletter
- Company News

In short, give them a reason to open your email. You're competing with everything else in their inbox.

How to Get Your Emails Read and Acted Upon

Congrats! You got your subscriber to open your email. But that was only one hurdle. Now you actually have to get your subscriber—er, reader—to take action. Here are some tips to increase your chances:

Use responsive templates. There's no one right way to make this happen, but one thing to keep in mind is that many of your subscribers will be looking at your email on their phone.

Don't believe me? Go look at your email metrics; they'll tell you what percentage of your subscribers are opening your email on a mobile device.

To satisfy both your mobile and desktop subscribers, you need to make sure your email is responsive. Email templates that tout themselves as "mobile" often look terrible on a desktop, so make sure the template is *responsive*. The best thing to do is send yourself a test copy and open it on both your phone and desktop computer.

Keep it short. People's attention spans are short...especially when they're on a mobile device. You need to quickly give them the reason why they should bother engaging with your content or clicking on your link.

Links should be easy to click on. Images should be easy to discern. Sentences should be short. Paragraphs should be all but non-existent.

Use images...except when you shouldn't. Most ESPs will tell you the value of images...how engaging they are and how they encourage people to click.

That's absolutely true.

Unfortunately, those images can also trigger Gmail--a very popular email service from Google--to move your email from the inbox and relegate it to the Promotions tab. That's like one step above the spam folder.

Both images and links high up in the email seem to trigger this response in Gmail, and often where Google goes, others follow.

If you want to improve open rates, you need to avoid the Promotions tab, which means no images and limit any links to the bottom of your email. However, many ESPs don't even offer a plain-text only email option, and they automatically include an unsubscribe link near the top...what's a marketer to do?

Like most things in life, there's a little bit of a tradeoff here. If you need to include images and links, do it. If you don't have to, search for an ESP that allows you to send out plain-text emails.

Make your calls to action obvious. Again, if you're looking for people to move from their inbox to your website, e-commerce store, or registration page, you need to make your calls to action obvious and easy to interact with.

Make sure your links are an obvious "action" color. Make sure buttons are big enough to click on. Repeat your call to action several times within the email.

How to Measure Your ROI

Your ESP will provide you with great statistics on how many subscribers you have, how many opened your email, how many clicked on it, and so forth. Combine this with the reports within Google Analytics to track how many people are visiting your site, filling out your contact form, registering for your event, etc., that can be tied back to your email marketing.

Takeaways

While the size of your list is important, don't lose sight of the true purpose of your list: to increase engagement and generate more leads.

Make sure your emails are delivered through an ESP, that they deliver on your subscribers' expectations, that they're formatted well, and that they include obvious calls to action.

Retargeting

It's happened to all of us. You're on Amazon, looking at garden hoses, but you don't end up buying anything. You head on over to Facebook and there's an ad for garden hoses. You want to catch up on the news and on CNN you see...garden hoses. You decide to jump the political divide and jump over to Fox News.

No luck, those garden hoses have found you there, too. It's like they're constantly on your trail, slithering up behind you.

It might have been a pair of boots on Zappos, or a Bed & Breakfast you discovered on TripAdvisor. Whatever the case, you've been "retargeted."

Here's how it works: you visit a website and the site drops a "cookie" on you. A cookie is a small piece of data that helps the website or advertiser remember a little bit of information about you.

These cookies are provided by retargeting companies like Adroll or Perfect Audience. In addition, large media companies like Google, Facebook, and Twitter offer their own retargeting solutions that appear on their sites and their partner sites.

Retargeting gets more sophisticated when you replace a cookie or update the information on a visitor.

For example, if someone goes to your jewelry site and buys a diamond necklace, you may not want to retarget them. (You might, to sell them a matching set of earrings, but I digress.) Showing ads to people who aren't likely to buy from you doesn't make a whole lot of sense. So you can set up your retargeting to not show these buyers ads going forward.

Another thing you can do is serve up different ads depending on which pages people visited. If you're selling real estate and someone looked at pages for waterfront homes, you could have ads that display your latest listings of waterfront homes.

Alternatively, if someone else visited pages about land for sale, you might show them ads featuring new lots that just came on the market.

Retargeting vs. Email Marketing

If the goal is to stay in front of your ideal customer while they're making a buying decision, both retargeting and email marketing have their strengths and weaknesses.

The nice thing about retargeting is that it doesn't require an action from your site visitor. Just by visiting your site, they have a little Spidey-tracker attached to their back. You can then serve up ads based on their visit or activity.

The nice thing about email marketing is that it *does* require an extra action from your site visitor. Whenever a prospect or customer actively moves forward, there's a certain level of commitment they have made to the process.

How to Get Started with Retargeting

Like ESPs in email marketing, there are companies that provide retargeting solutions. At flyte, we currently use Adroll because it is able to serve ads up on the general web and on Facebook.

In general, these retargeting companies will provide you with a snippet of code that needs to be placed on all of your pages. You can then segment your audience based on which pages they visit, and even release them from retargeting ads if they take a desired action on your site.

Most retargeting companies require up-front payment, and then spend your ad dollars over the course of a week or month. There isn't a bidding process like in Adwords.

All these companies offer robust reporting tools so that you can determine your ROI.

Social Media

Social media is one way to keep the lines of conversation going, even after someone's left your site.

You can encourage them to like you on Facebook, follow you on Twitter, or become LinkedIn with you. They may check out your podcast or subscribe to your YouTube channel.

All of these things are great. If they actually take those actions. Sending someone to Facebook doesn't ensure that they'll like your page, even if you send them directly to your page. It does ensure, however, that they're no longer at your site.

When clients come to me to build a new website, often a major concern is that it will integrate with social media. And by that, they mean that they will create pathways from their website to social media sites that are more active, more engaging, and more fun than their own site.

I would recommend that entrepreneurs use their energy to get people off of popular social media sites and onto their own site, rather than the other way around.

While there's no harm in including links to social sites, I'd recommend having the link open in a popup or modal window to keep the visitor at your site.

Of the three methods for retention—email marketing, retargeting, and social media—social media is the most tenuous.

Wrapping Up

Only a small fraction of site visitors will take a desired action while they're at your website. Many of them are just there to do research and are not ready to make a buying decision. Once they leave, they're gone for good—unless you can find a way to stay in communication.

There are three main ways to retain their attention:

- **Email marketing:** Use a lead magnet to entice a site visitor into providing you their email address and giving you access to their inbox
- **Retargeting:** Advertise to people who have already visited your website and are likely interested in your products and services
- **Social:** Get visitors to like, follow, or connect with you on social media so you can keep the conversation going.

By leveraging these three techniques, you can build brand awareness and trust and increase the chances that your site visitor will return to do business with you.

Evaluate

Half the money I spend on advertising is wasted; the trouble is, I don't know which half.

—John Wanamaker

One of the best things about digital marketing is that you can really track a lot of your activity and spend to see if it's providing a positive ROI for your business.

While not everything can be tracked—a tweet might increase your brand exposure to someone that will later cause them to Google you—there is a lot of data that can be reviewed so that you can continually make improvements in your marketing.

Evaluating the effectiveness of your digital marketing comes down to measuring and analyzing the data.

The most important tool that any small business has to evaluate their digital marketing is Google Analytics. Google Analytics is a free tool that generates reams of data about your site visitors: how they found you, where they came from, what pages they visited, and what they did before leaving your site.

Beyond Google Analytics, most social media platforms have their own metrics you can review, both for organic activity and ads. Also, your ESP can provide metrics around deliveries, opens, and clicks.

By spending some time each week evaluating your activity, you'll continually get better results.

URL Builder

Before jumping into Google Analytics, let's talk about an incredibly powerful tool that makes Google Analytics even better.

It's another tool from Google call the URL Builder. Even if you've never used it, you may have seen it in action. If you've ever clicked on a link in an email or in social media and seen a really long URL like http://www.theagentsofchange.com/?utm_source=twtrb&utm_medium=twitter&utm_campaign=eb in your browser window, then you have been on the receiving end of it.

The URL Builder gives you additional tracking information. The tool is free, with the only cost being a small investment in your time.

I don't put every URL that I share through the URL builder, but if I'm running a specific campaign, I definitely invest the time.

How to Use URL Builder

To access the URL Builder visit theleadmachinebook.com/URLBuilder.

Once you're there, scroll down to find the URL Builder Form. In the Website URL field, enter the URL you're trying to drive traffic to.

In the Campaign Source field, you want to enter the source, or where you plan on putting the link. Some possible solutions are Facebook, email newsletter, or a local newspaper's website.

In the Campaign Medium field, you want to enter the marketing medium you used. Banner ads, social media, and email are all options.

I don't know about you, but I sometimes feel there's a lot of overlap between Source and Medium. The most important thing is to be consistent in what you put in these fields.

The next two fields are Term and Content, which are optional and generally I don't use.

The last field is Campaign Name, which is what you're going to call the campaign.

In the example above, the Source is twtrb. That's our shorthand for my Twitter account at @therichbrooks.

The Medium is Twitter.

Primary Dimension: **Campaign** Source Medium Source / Medium Other ▾			
Plot Rows Secondary dimension ▾ Sort Type: Default ▾			
	Acquisition		
Campaign ?	Sessions ? ↓	% New Sessions ?	New Users ?
	6,148 % of Total: 18.83% (32,649)	**76.69%** Avg for View: 79.42% (-3.44%)	**4,715** % of Total: 18.18% (25,931)
1. Conference	**1,394** (22.67%)	96.13%	**1,340** (28.42%)
2. eb	**889** (14.46%)	68.84%	**612** (12.98%)
3. aoc	**541** (8.80%)	69.32%	**375** (7.95%)
4. rebsome	**439** (7.14%)	82.69%	**363** (7.70%)
5. AgentsOfChange	**325** (5.29%)	95.08%	**309** (6.55%)
6. AdEspresso Newsletter	**312** (5.07%)	70.83%	**221** (4.69%)
7. aoc2016	**288** (4.68%)	52.43%	**151** (3.20%)
8. rebblkfriday	**282** (4.59%)	80.14%	**226** (4.79%)
9. buffer	**198** (3.22%)	71.21%	**141** (2.99%)
10. rebmob	**190** (3.09%)	82.11%	**156** (3.31%)

The Campaign is eb, which is short for early bird.

I used this URL when I posted links about the Agents of Change in my personal Twitter account. When I later look at Google Analytics, I can measure the ROI of these links against other campaigns we've run.

Build a Spreadsheet

You may have more than one person who works on a campaign, so it's important to be consistent in how you're using the URL builder. If one person calls the Medium "banner" and another "banners" and still another splits them into "skyscraper" and "horizontal_ad", your reports are going to be a mess and provide no additional insight.

Before starting your campaign, you should build a spreadsheet of what you're going to enter into your URL Builder. Break it up into Campaign, Source, and Name. Then it's a simple matter of people copying and pasting the correct element into each field for consistency.

I've shared a Google Spreadsheet we use for Agents of Change so that you can see how to model your own. Just visit theleadmachinebook.com/URLspreadsheet to access it.

Google Analytics

If you only use one tool to measure your results, use this one. When someone calls me up looking for a new website or some marketing help, I always ask for access to their Google Analytics.

If they don't have Google Analytics installed, I ask them to get it installed (or I do it myself), and let it run for a couple of weeks before I put together a proposal. This is because, without looking at the data, we don't really know what the underlying problems are.

I've had many conversations with entrepreneurs who believe that their problem is lack of search traffic, only to discover their search traffic was fine. The problem might instead be a high bounce rate (when someone visits just one page on your site and "bounces" away), or a very low conversion rate (the percentage of people who take a measurable, desired action).

There's so much to Google Analytics; so many reports, so many configurations, so many options, that it can feel overwhelming. To keep this simple, I'm going to focus on the best way to set up Google Analytics, the most important reports to look at, and how to use those reports to improve your SEO and other digital marketing.

I'm also going to share some pro tips along the way.

Setting Up Google Analytics... the Right Way

If you don't have Google Analytics set up, don't worry. It's fairly straightforward and I'm going to walk you through how to do it in this chapter.

I'm also going to show you how to set up Analytics "right." And by that I mean that most people just install the code and do nothing else. With a few extra steps, you can turn your Google Analytics into an incredibly powerful tool.

Setting up Your Google Analytics Account

Google Analytics needs to be associated with a Google account. This can be an existing account, such as your Gmail address, or one you've set up specifically for your company's web presence.

I recommend the latter. As your business grows, other people are going to need access to different parts of your Google account: Analytics, YouTube, Business Listings, etc. Or, if you're working for someone else, you may move on and you don't want your account tied to your previous job. Just create a new account like myonlinebusiness@gmail.com and then you can have everything forwarded to your main Gmail address, or other email if you prefer.

What I strongly recommend against is having your web developer put the analytics under his account. Some developers do this because it's easier for them, some because they're evil. Well, maybe not evil, but they definitely have control issues.

If they add your domain under their account, then you are stuck with them. If you ever decide to leave, you have to leave all those analytics behind and start with a fresh account. Also, they can't give you full control of your analytics, because that would give you access to all of their other clients as well.

The best thing you can do is get your own Google Analytics account and provide them with administrative access so they can generate and install the code, run reports, add filters, and all the other important things they need to accomplish for you.

Installing the Code

In Google Analytics' admin you'll see a three column hierarchy: Account, Property, View.

Account is basically your business. Property is your website. If you have multiple websites, you'll have multiple properties. View is different views of the analytics for each property. You may set up a view just to view traffic from your own country, or a view that filters out traffic from your company, or a view that only looks at your store traffic.

It's important to realize that Google Analytics cannot travel through time. In other words, it doesn't start working until you install it on your website; it can't see what happened before it got there. The sooner you get it installed, the sooner you can start tracking your traffic.

Under the Property column, you'll see Tracking Info, and under that, Tracking Code. There is a snippet of code there that needs to be placed on every page you want to track. If you're using a CMS like WordPress, you or your developer can include it in the page code so that every page on your site and every page going forward will have that code with no additional work required.

Setting up Users

Chances are, more than just one person will want or need access to your analytics, especially if you're working with outside developers or marketers. You may want to give specific people more or less access to your analytics, depending on their needs.

Again, under Properties, you'll see User Management. By clicking on this link you'll be able to add, edit, or delete users, as well as give them levels of access to your account.

As a reminder, it's best for your developer to use your own Google account to create your analytics and then add himself as a user.

If you're not seeing the ability to add or edit users, it may mean that you don't have enough privileges yourself and someone else is in control of your analytics.

Setting up Filters

You can filter out some types of traffic. The most common use of filters is to hide your own activity on your website. If you are spending a lot of time at your own site, updating information, for example, you don't want your activity skewing your analytics. Here's how you filter out any activity coming from your company.

Under Views click on Filters. Click on the red Add Filter button. If you don't see this button, it means you don't have enough privileges and this account may be owned by someone else.

On the next screen give your filter a name. If it's to filter out office traffic, you could call it Office Traffic. Your filter type will be Predefined. Using the three pulldown menus, choose to "Exclude" "traffic from the IP addresses" "that are equal to" and then enter your IP address in the next field.

If you don't know what your IP address is, just Google "what is my IP address?" Just make sure you're doing it from the location where you want to filter out the traffic from. Otherwise you might just be filtering out traffic from the local Starbucks!

Google will give you a response which you can copy and paste into that field. Save your work and you're all set.

Edit Filter

Filter Information

Filter Name

| Office Traffic |

Filter Type

| Predefined | Custom |

| Exclude ▾ | traffic from the IP addresses ▾ | that are equal to ▾ |

IP address

| |

Repeat for your home office if you wish.

Get Rid of Bad Bots

At the time of this writing, there are spam bots that will ping your site and then ricochet away. They don't do you any harm, but they do mess with your analytics, skewing your results.

Google Analytics doesn't have a great response to this, but they do offer a checkbox you can and should select. Under View and View Settings you'll see a box called Bot Filtering. Go ahead and check it, filtering out all known bots and spiders.

This isn't a perfect solution, but it does help.

Set up Goals

If you're trying to determine how effective your digital marketing is, it's critical to set up Goals. Goals help you uncover how much of your traffic is converting, and where your best traffic is coming from.

There are many types of goals Google Analytics can track, including whether people are spending a desired amount of time on your site, whether they are visiting a minimum number of pages, or whether they registered at the site.

The most common goal, however, is a destination goal: in other words, did they arrive at a specific page? This is a great way of determining whether they filled out a contact form or signed up for an email newsletter.

The easiest way to measure this is to send someone to a unique thank you page after completing this step. Then you can use Google Analytics to measure this as a completed Goal.

Some forms don't actually move someone to a new page when they complete the form. This makes it technically more difficult to measure your results.

Assuming that your email registration or contact form sends someone to a new page, this is how you can set up a simple Goal:

- Choose Goals in the Views column
- Choose Custom and continue
- Give your Goal a descriptive name, i.e., Contact Form or Email Registration
- Under Type, choose Destination and continue
- Under Goals Detail enter in the thank you page URL
- Optionally, add a value to the goal*
- If you want to track multiple steps to the goal, you can add that information by selecting Funnel

* I find adding a value to a goal very helpful, even if it's a best guess. What is the lifetime value of a customer? $500? $5,000? $50,000? How many people who complete your forms tend to become a customer? One in five? One in ten? One in a hundred?

Based on the idea that a customer's lifetime value for your business is $5,000, and one in ten people who fill out your form becomes a customer, the value for that goal is $500.

Connect Your Account to Search Console

Google's Search Console, formerly Webmaster Tools, is a powerful reporting tool for site owners. You can connect Search Console to your analytics to bring all of those reports into Analytics.

Under Property, click on Property Settings. Scroll down to the bottom and click on the link Adjust Search Console. On the next page you should see your domain under the Search Console listing, assuming it's under the same Google account. Save this, and now you get all the power of Search Console in your Google Analytics.

If you don't have your site in Search Console, you'll need to visit theleadmachinebook.com/searchconsole. (Or just Google "search console.")

Congrats!

Congratulations! Your Google Analytics are all set up and optimized. If you installed Google Analytics for the first time, you can check your analytics in 24-48 hours to see if you're collecting any data. However, you might want to wait a couple of weeks before taking any of your reports too seriously. A few days of reporting isn't statistically significant. An email blast or a link from a popular blog could really skew your reports if they're that young.

A Quick Tour of Google Analytics

About a month or so after we've launched a new website, I give our clients a tour of their Google Analytics. This allows time for the dust to settle and for us to get a better picture of what's working and not working at the site.

While each tour is unique, I'd like to give you a similar tour in this chapter. We'll take a look at some of the most important features in Google Analytics and some of the reports you should be paying attention to right out of the gate.

Your Tour Starts Here

Once you've logged into Google Analytics, you're taken to the home page. This lists all of your accounts, whether you have one or a hundred. By selecting your website, you're taken to the Reporting section.

The left hand column has 8 items:

- Dashboards
- Shortcuts
- Intelligence Events
- Real-Time
- Audience
- Acquisition
- Behavior
- Conversions

As a small business owner or marketer, most of your time will be spent in the bottom four tabs, so let's focus on those. In fact, Google Analytics takes you to Audience > Overview.

By default, Google Analytics shows you the previous 30 days of activity, broken down by day. However, like almost everything in Google Analytics, that can be changed.

In the top right corner, you'll see a pulldown menu with the range of the last 30 days on it. By clicking on the date range, you'll see a three-month calendar and the current date range. Using either of these, you can change the start and end date of reporting.

You can look at the past 24 hours, the past week, or the past 365 days. Just choose the date range and click Apply. No matter what page or report you navigate to in Google Analytics, your new date range will "stick," impacting all of your reporting.

Google Analytics even allows you to compare one date with another. This is helpful if you want to see how this March compared with the previous March for your business, or this month compared with last month.

Again, this side-by-side comparison will stick until you change the dates again, or sign out of your session.

Audience

The Audience reports are all about who's visiting your website. Not by name, or even email address, but by demographics and other criteria.

There are many reports within Audience (and an infinite number of variations thanks to the ability to tweak date ranges, add filters, and change variables), but let's focus on just a few here.

Overview: Overview will give you a quick snapshot of your site traffic. How many sessions (times people visited your website), users, page views, etc.

It will also provide you with your Bounce Rate: the number of people who visited just one page on your site and then left. Generally, you hope this number will be low, but if you have an active blog, many people may just come for a single article and then leave.

Like all reports, there's as much in the interpretation as there is in the data. For some sites, bounce rate is incredibly important, for other sites not so much.

Demographics: You'll need to agree to share more of your data with Google to turn on these reports, but they will provide you with a snapshot of your audience, broken down by age and gender.

Geo > Location: Some businesses need to know where their customers are coming from, for others it doesn't matter. For an inn in Bar Harbor, they may be interested in knowing if there are pockets within the U.S. where they are getting a lot of traffic. This may help with targeting future ad campaigns.

For a Detroit bagel shop, they may want to see if a surge in site traffic is due to local customers, or if suddenly they're getting a surge of unimportant traffic from Bangladesh.

Even if this doesn't impact your business, seeing where traffic is coming form is visually intriguing. In this report, you start with a map of the Earth. The darker blue colors of some countries relate to the amount of traffic that country is sending your way.

If you click on a country, say the US, you'll then get a breakdown by state. Again, the darker blue states represent more traffic. You can even click within each state to see approximately where those people live or work.

Mobile: Mobile is becoming a more important component of every business website. You can see what percentage of your traffic is still coming from a desktop compared to tablet and smartphone traffic.

Acquisition

The Acquisition reports are all about how people found you.

All Traffic > Channels: Google Analytics breaks down your traffic by a number of different channels, including:

- Organic Search (traffic from search)
- Direct (people typing in your domain or having book-marked you)
- Referral (people clicking on a link to your site)
- Social (traffic from social media sites)
- Email (traffic from email programs)
- And more

Adwords: These reports cover your Adwords campaigns and how effective they are. They show no activity if you're not currently running PPC on Google.

Search Console: This section shows the reports that Google is pulling from your search console assuming you've connected Analytics to Search Console.

Search Console > Landing Pages: Here you'll find your most popular landing pages (the first page someone hits on your site), as well as information on how many times people saw this page as a search result (Impressions), how many times they clicked through (Clicks), what the average search result ranking is for each landing page, as well as additional information.

If you've set up Goals, you can also see how these landing pages are performing for you. If you have a high converting page, you may want to work on optimizing that page more for the search engines, either by improving the page title, or getting more incoming links to that page, or some other tactic.

Search Console > Queries: This report provides similar information, but rather than focusing on the pages people land on, it focuses on the searches they just performed.

By default, Google Analytics shows you the top 10 results per page. However, you can increase this to up to 5,000 responses. I recommend increasing your results to 100 and then skimming through the results. You may start to see some trends that will give you insight into what type of searches are pulling up your site as a result. By improving the optimization of pages on your site that may be a result for this content, you can increase your qualified traffic.

Social: This report will show you a breakdown of how much traffic you got from different social sites, and if you set up Goals with a value attached, the value they represent to your business. It will also show you Contributed Social Conversion vs. Last Interaction Social Conversion.

What this means is that if someone visits your site because of a social interaction, but they don't complete a goal, but then come back later and do complete a goal, that's a Contributed Social Conversion. If they convert right after coming from a social site, that's marked as a Last Interaction.

Campaigns > All Campaigns: This is where all that information that you put into your URL builder comes into play. You can get great information on which campaigns, mediums, and sources are driving the best, highest converting traffic to your site.

The default view is Campaigns, but you can change that to Medium or Source, or Source / Medium, if you want to get more granular with your information.

If you've attached values to your Goals, you can quickly see which campaign, medium, or source has generated the most value for your business.

Behavior

The reports in Behavior tell you what actions people took when they were at your site.

Behavior > Behavior Flow: This is an important, but potentially confusing report. It aims to show you how people navigate and opt out of your website. What I find it best for is finding big leaks in your traffic flow.

By default, this report shows you your most popular landing pages. By rolling over the boxes that represent each page, you can see which traffic moves on to other pages and which ones leave your site. If you find a popular landing page that's losing a lot of traffic, you should work on improving this page.

Site Content: This report breaks down the most popular pages on your website. Generally, the most popular page is your home page, represented by the /. If a different page is your most popular page, you may want to investigate why that is.

Occasionally, a very popular blog post that has a more general appeal than the rest of our content will beat out our home page. If it's too general or off-topic, I recommend ignoring it.

If it aligns with your offerings, then I recommend you create a targeted lead magnet to encourage people to join your mailing list.

Site Speed > Page Timings: Site speed is becoming a more important metric all the time. Not only does a slow loading page increase the chances that someone will click away out of frustration, it impacts how your page ranks in Google search. Google is looking to provide the most valuable resources for each search, and a slow-loading page is deemed less valuable.

However, as you look through this report, you may notice that many of your most popular, most viewed pages and posts are also the slowest-loading. That's often because they're deeper content with more images or other resources.

Still, if you have a well performing page that is also slow to load, look at how you can improve that page's speed to get even better results.

Site Speed > Speed Suggestions: In this report, you'll see suggestions for each page on how you can improve the load time.

Conversions

The reports in this section provide information on how much of your website traffic is converting or taking desired, measurable steps down the sales funnel.

Goals > Overview: This will give you a quick snapshot of how your site is converting people to buy, fill out forms, or sign up for your email newsletter, among other Goals you have set up.

It's nice to have the overview of your Goals in one place, although I find the breakdown you get in the Acquisition section more helpful for making decisions.

Takeaways

Google Analytics is a critical tool in understanding the effectiveness of your digital marketing. Because it's free, simple to install, and easy to use, there's no excuse not to be using it.

If you can carve out just fifteen minutes a week or set up automatic reports to be delivered to you regularly, you're well on your way to better understanding the impact different campaigns are having on your bottom line.

Evaluating Your Email Marketing

As I've mentioned before, email marketing is one of the most important elements of a successful digital marketing campaign.

Getting someone onto your email list can be considered a lead in and of itself. It's a measurable result that gives you permission to "gently" market to someone.

It's also a step further towards generating a more significant lead and even making a sale.

Even though you can—and should—use URL Builder in your links that you include in your email blasts and newsletters, you can still measure other important aspects of your email marketing to improve your results.

Here are some KPIs that you should be tracking:

- **List Size:** While list size isn't the only important metric, you can't deny its significance. Some people have a very successful, very engaged subscriber base that's not very large, however, in *general* with a larger list you can reach more people. The important thing here is to see if your list is growing.

- **Open Rate:** What percentage of people are opening your email? Your ESP will provide information on the open rate for every email campaign you send. Each industry has its own open rate average. Sometimes your ESP will provide that information, but if they don't, you should be able to google it.

- **Click Rate:** Opens are one thing, but click throughs to your site are important if you're looking for people to take action. Are there certain types of emails that get better click through rates? Look at a bunch of your recent emails and see if you can spot a trend.

If you have several calls to action that all go to the same page within an email, and want to see which one was clicked on the most, you can use URL Builder and give each one a unique value, whether it's Source or Name. Just remember, URL Builder is about being consistent, so break out that spreadsheet!

Evaluating Your Social Media

There are a lot of things you can measure in social media. How many likes you got. How many connections you have on LinkedIn. How many people follow you on Twitter. How many people download each episode of your podcast. How many subscribers you have on your YouTube channel.

Also, almost every platform has its own metrics. Facebook, Twitter, YouTube, and Pinterest. The list goes on. Each one can give you insights into how you can get a larger audience and get better engagement, if you know how to read the tea leaves and take action.

As far as generating leads, however, you should be focused on getting people to your website, and to a specific squeeze page if possible. While it's important to look at the different social media analytics, especially if you're generating a lot of traffic from a specific site, or if you know your audience hangs out on the site, never lose sight of your true goal: generating more leads.

Likes are not leads. Follows are not leads. Even comments and shares are not leads. These have other benefits. They help build your brand. They help you reach a wider audience. They help build trust. They are all in service of you generating more leads and sales for your business.

My recommendation is to identify the platforms that are most promising in terms of traffic and leads and focus your attention there.

In Closing

As I said at the beginning of the book, I don't expect you to put all of these strategies and tactics into place all at once. In fact, that's a recipe for failure.

Instead, start by making sure you've built a website that is designed for results. A site that is mobile-friendly, easy-to-update, and will scale with your business. A site that will convert visitors into customers.

From there, use the strategies and tactics that are likely to drive traffic. Continually optimize your site, create new blog posts, podcasts, or videos, and promote them through social media. Invest in some digital advertising.

To retain your connection with your ideal customers, get them to sign up for your email list, or follow them around the web with retargeting.

And of course, measure and evaluate your activity. Everything I've written in this book is based upon my experience and the experience of our hundreds of customers. These are the best practices as I know them. However, YMMV. You may find a tactic I dismissed works well for you, or vice versa. You have to measure and evaluate what you're doing if you want to see continued success.

The world is changing, and industry by industry, more research and information gathering is being done online and through mobile devices. If for some strange reason your industry hasn't been rocked by digital, your time is coming. It doesn't matter if you're B2B. It doesn't matter if your clients are older, or unplugged. More and more people are using the internet to make decisions to use you or your competitor than ever before.

By using the strategies and tactics in this book, I hope you find your way to more visibility, traffic, and leads online.

And if any of tactics in this book work for you, or if you have any questions, feel free to reach out to me on Twitter at @therich-brooks or send me an email via our online form at http://www.takeflyte.com/contact

Trust me, it'll reach me, and you won't even have to wrestle a CAPTCHA.

Acronyms

B2B - Business to Business

B2C - Business to Consumer

BBB - Better Business Bureau

CIP - Content Intake Packet

CLV - Customer Lifetime Value

CMS - Content Management System

CRM - Customer Relationship Manager

CTA - Call to Action

CTR - Click Through Rate

ESP - Email Service Provider

IRL - In Real Life

ISP - Internet Service Provider

KPI - Key Performance Indicators

MLS - Multi-Listing Service

OSE - Open Site Explorer

PCI - Payment Card Industry

ROI - Return on Investment

RSS - Real Simple Syndication

RWD - Responsive Web Design

SEO - Search Engine Optimization

VA - Virtual Assistant

WYSIWYG - What You See Is What You Get

YMMV - Your Mileage May Vary

Acknowledgements

No book is written solely by the author. The author is merely the typist.

Thank you to my fellow crew members at flyte new media. You've inspired me to be the best I can be over the past twenty years, and you've always done your best to help other small businesses grow through the internet.

Thank you to my clients and customers, who have provided me with the challenges, feedback, and insights that allowed me to put this book together.

Thank you to the 170 plus digital marketing experts who have come on The Agents of Change podcast over the past few years to fill my head with amazing strategies and tactics.

I couldn't have done it without Julie Ann Eason, my friend and book coach, who shepherded me through the whole process. She is an amazing asset to any author, new or experienced.

Thank you to my parents, Bob and Marilyn Brooks, who put up with me for so many years. They saw the potential that I myself didn't even see. If you want to get a very funny, very sweet insight into what raising Rich Brooks was really like, my dad spoke on this topic as he introduced me at The Agents of Change Digital Marketing Conference in 2016. [theleadmachinebook.com/afathersburden]

Finally, I'd like to thank my wife, Cybele, and my daughters, Maya and Sophie, for their support and understanding while I undertook this journey.

manew

61546944R00178

Made in the USA
Lexington, KY
13 March 2017